LOCKE'S PHILOSOPHY OF LANGUAGE

This book examines John Locke's claims about the nature and workings of language. Walter Ott proposes a new interpretation of Locke's thesis that words signify ideas in the mind of the speaker, and argues that rather than employing such notions as sense or reference, Locke relies on an ancient tradition that understands signification as reliable indication. He then uses this interpretation to explain crucial areas of Locke's metaphysics and epistemology, including essence, abstraction, knowledge, and mental representation. His discussion, which is the first book-length treatment of its topic, challenges many of the current orthodox readings of Locke, and will be of interest to historians of philosophy and philosophers of language alike.

WALTER R. OTT is Assistant Professor of Philosophy at East Tennessee State University. He has published in a number of journals including *Ancient Philosophy*, *Dialogue*, and *Locke Studies / Locke Newsletter*.

LOCKE'S PHILOSOPHY OF LANGUAGE

WALTER R. OTT

East Tennessee State University

CAMBRIDGE
UNIVERSITY PRESS

PUBLISHED BY THE PRESS SYNDICATE OF THE UNIVERSITY OF CAMBRIDGE
The Pitt Building, Trumpington Street, Cambridge, United Kingdom

CAMBRIDGE UNIVERSITY PRESS
The Edinburgh Building, Cambridge, CB2 2RU, UK
40 West 20th Street, New York, NY 10011–4211, USA
477 Williamstown Road, Port Melbourne, VIC 3207, Australia
Ruiz de Alarcón 13, 28014 Madrid, Spain
Dock House, The Waterfront, Cape Town 8001, South Africa

http://www.cambridge.org

© Walter R. Ott 2004

First published 2004

Printed in the United Kingdom at the University Press, Cambridge

Typeface Adobe Garamond 11/12.5 pt.   *System* LaTeX 2_ε [TB]

A catalogue record for this book is available from the British Library

Library of Congress Cataloguing in Publication data
Ott, Walter R.
Locke's philosophy of language / Walter R. Ott.
p.   cm.
Includes bibliographical references and index.
ISBN 0 521 83119 9
1. Locke, John, 1632–1704 – Contributions in philosophy of language.   2. Language and
languages – Philosophy.   I. Title.
P85.L58O88   2003
121′.68′092 – dc21   2003048988

ISBN 0 521 83119 9 hardback

Contents

Acknowledgements

I would like to thank the following people for their help with this book. Two anonymous reviewers for Cambridge University Press provided helpful comments. Hugh LaFollette and Christopher Panza commented on particular chapters. Jorge Secada, Dan Devereux, Harold Langsam, Mitch Green, and others at the University of Virginia commented on earlier versions of one, two, four, five, and six. I had helpful discussions on these issues with Rebecca Hanrahan, Paul Tudico and Michael Pelczar. Finally, Marshie Agee suggested corrections and improvements to the entire manuscript.

Like everyone interested in Locke, I am indebted to Roland Hall, but I am particularly so for his permission to reprint material from my "Locke's Argument from Signification" (*Locke Studies*, 2002) in chapter four. Portions of my "Propositional Attitudes in Modern Philosophy" (*Dialogue*, 2002) appear in chapter two. Part of chapter one appeared in a different form in the *Journal of Philosophical Research* (2002).

I would also like to thank Hilary Gaskin of Cambridge University Press for her guidance and encouragement. Thanks to Alan D. Robinson for the portrait of Locke, and to Angus and Malcolm for inspiration.

Note on textual references

LOCKE

References to the *Essay* are to Locke (1975) and follow the standard form: Book, chapter, section: page number. Thus 'III.ix.21: 488' refers to Book III, chapter ix, section 21, page 488.

BERKELEY

All references are to the edition of A.A. Luce and T.E. Jessop (1949–58). When citing the *Principles*, the numbers given refer to paragraphs; when citing the *Philosophical Commentaries*, the reference is to a number entry. When other works are cited, the reference is to the page number of the relevant volume in Luce and Jessop. The following abbreviations have been used in the text:

NTV: *New Theory of Vision*
PC: *Philosophical Commentaries*
PI: the published (as opposed to manuscript) introduction to the *Treatise Concerning the Principles of Human Knowledge*
P: Part I of the *Treatise Concerning the Principles of Human Knowledge*
TD: *Three Dialogues between Hylas and Philonous*
ALC: *Alciphron, or the Minute Philosopher*
TVV: *The Theory of Vision Vindicated and Explained*

Introduction

> I must confess then, that when I first began this Discourse of the Understanding, and a good while after, I had not the least Thought, that any Consideration of Words was at all necessary to it. But when having passed over the Original and Composition of our *Ideas*, I began to examine the Extent and Certainty of our Knowledge, I found it had so near a connexion with Words, that unless their force and manner of Signification were first well observed, there could be very little said clearly and pertinently concerning Knowledge . . .
>
> (III.ix.21: 488)

Despite the importance Locke attaches to issues of language, this aspect of his philosophy has drawn comparatively little attention in the secondary literature. One reason for this neglect might be the disfavor into which what is commonly understood as his view has fallen. Locke is regarded as a "mentalist" who has been refuted by the arguments of Frege, Wittgenstein, Putnam, and their followers. Haven't we learned that meanings aren't in the head? Why bother with Locke at all?

One justification historians of philosophy are apt to give in such contexts is that the view in question has simply been the victim of uncharitable interpretation. This has certainly been the case with Locke's philosophy of language, from his day down to our own. Locke is not vulnerable to the standard arguments deployed against him, and his main rival, the causal theory of reference, is simply false (or so I shall argue). Examining Locke's philosophy of language is more than a mere antiquarian enterprise, and I shall argue that he has much to teach us. At the same time, I shall not hesitate to convict Locke of error when I find it. I do not hold the currently fashionable position that one can only justifiably attribute a view to a great dead philosopher when that view is, by our lights, true, or at least plausible.[1]

---

[1] For an instance of the tendency to insist that fidelity of interpretation requires the ascription of what are currently considered plausible views, see David Behan (2000). For a corrective, see John Yolton (2000), a reply to Behan.

I

As the epigraph indicates, Locke was not engaged in a disinterested inquiry into the nature of language. His reflections on epistemology and metaphysics drove him to explore language to a much greater degree than he had initially intended (see I.i.3: 44). I shall show that many of the key issues in Locke's philosophy turn in part on his theory of meaning. By this I do not mean to suggest that philosophy of language is foundational for Locke in the way it is for, say, Quine or Wittgenstein. My point is only that, as Locke himself came to see in the course of writing the *Essay*, the project of investigating the nature and limits of knowledge cannot be divorced from an inquiry into the workings of language. What is more, such an inquiry has consequences for metaphysics, since some metaphysical positions (such as those of the Aristotelians) are generated by a failure to appreciate the purposes and capacities of language.

On Locke's view, language allows us to reveal our minds to one another. Since we cannot immediately perceive anyone else's ideas or mental acts, we require some medium through which communication can take place. But precisely because this is such a common occurrence in everyday life, language can bewitch us. In particular, we can be tempted to regard words as somehow directly latching onto things rather than merely indicating ideas in the speaker's mind. Locke gives a careful analysis of the forces that might drive us to suppose that words signify things or real essences rather than ideas, a position he regards as absurd.

In addition to allowing him to clarify his position on such vexed topics as substance and real essence, Locke thinks a careful discussion of language will yield anti-Aristotelian results. Locke sets out to expose fundamental confusions in the positions of his chief antagonists and takes his place in a tradition that runs through Bacon and Hobbes. Unlike these figures, however, Locke presents a developed position on the nature of language and uses it to undermine, in novel ways, the "learned Gibberish" of the Schoolmen. His philosophy of language has normative force: he wishes to explore not only *how* language is used but also how it *should* be used.

We should not assume that Locke is concerned to account for all uses of language. His focus is squarely on language as it figures in philosophy and science. Locke is often abused for neglecting the complexities of language use; he has nothing to say, for example, about performative utterances such as promising, or emotive or prescriptive language. Berkeley was perhaps the first to take him to task for this, and his critique is well taken. Nevertheless, Locke's view should be judged according to whether it is a satisfactory account of those admittedly narrow areas of language in which he was interested.

INTERPRETATIVE DIFFICULTIES

Locke's philosophy of language centers around what I shall call his "linguistic thesis": the claim that words signify ideas. This is meaningless, of course, unless we have some notion of what "idea" is to mean. The controversy over this question seems interminable; the Port-Royalians' claim that "the word 'idea' is one of those that are so clear that they cannot be explained by others, because none is more clear or simple" seems comical in retrospect.[2]

Locke introduces his use of the term thus: "*Idea* . . . serves best to stand for whatsoever is the Object of the Understanding when a Man thinks" (I.i.8: 47). In this use, at least, an idea is an intentional object. Other evidence in the *Essay* and elsewhere suggests that Lockean ideas are mental items or contents. Since "the Things, the Mind contemplates, are none of them, besides itself, present to the Understanding, 'tis necessary that something else, as a Sign or Representation of the thing it considers, should be present to it: And these are *Ideas*" (IV.xxi.4: 720–1). Ideas (mental objects) must be posited in order to explain the mind's ability to think about anything other than itself. Locke requires that the immediate objects of thought be "ontologically present" to the mind, to use Michael Ayers's phrase.[3] It follows that only mental objects can be the immediate objects of thought. This line of thought is apparent in Locke's attack on his Aristotelian critic John Sergeant. In a letter to Stillingfleet, Locke argues that Sergeant's direct realism has the absurd consequence that physical objects are literally in the mind (see chapter six). The requirement of ontological presence makes representationalism (or idealism) inescapable.

This introduces a terminological difficulty it would be well to clear up. "Intentional object" is ambiguous between the idea and what it represents; both clearly fit the description "object of thought." I shall restrict my use of this phrase to ideas, using the admittedly cumbersome locution "extra-mental objects" for the ultimate rather than the immediate object of thought.

I have said that I follow Locke's text (I.i.8: 47) in treating ideas as objects. Nevertheless, Locke suggests later in the *Essay* that some ideas (such as ideas of relations) involve mental acts as well as ideas. Indeed, I shall argue below that Locke's semiotic empiricism requires him to extend his use of "idea" to include complexes of acts and objects.

---

[2] Arnauld and Nicole (1996, p. 25). I do not mean to suggest that the Port-Royalians themselves are unclear on the meaning of '*idée*.'

[3] See Ayers (1986).

The above is at best a start at characterizing the role ideas have to play in Locke's position; it says nothing about the *nature* of Lockean ideas. Although Michael Ayers's claim that Locke construes ideas as images is quite plausible, for the purposes of my arguments, I can remain neutral on this debate.[4]

Quite apart from the controversy over ideas, Locke's inconsistent use of terminology where language is concerned means that any interpretation will have to reconcile apparently contradictory statements. For instance, although Locke says that words signify nothing but ideas, he also says that words *primarily* signify nothing but ideas, suggesting that in some other sense words signify extra-mental objects. He sometimes claims that words "name" things, but he also says often enough that words name ideas only. In chapter one, I set out a number of interpretative options, listing the cost of each, and begin to make a case for my own view, according to which secondary signification and other linguistic notions are reducible to primary signification or signification *simpliciter*. Despite Locke's use of words like "denominate," "mark," "designate," and "design," I argue that signification is his fundamental linguistic notion. I suggest ways in which his use of these other words might be reconciled with this claim.

PLAN OF THE BOOK

The project has two goals: first, to explicate and assess Locke's philosophy of language, and second, to use this new interpretation to explore other areas of his philosophy, including his arguments against the Aristotelians and his views on mental representation, abstraction, essence, knowledge, and skepticism.

Locke's doctrines about language have been widely misunderstood. Locke does not hold that words refer to ideas, that ideas serve as the sense of words (which in turn refer to things), or that words "express" ideas but refer to things. Instead, words indicate ideas in the mind of the speaker. In the first chapter, I argue for this interpretation by examining a tradition of understanding signification that runs through such figures as Aristotle, the Stoics, and Hobbes. Although this tradition typically focuses on *ideas* or sensations as indicators (in this case, of extra-mental objects), it also deploys signification in its account of the workings of language. In Locke's case, both words and ideas are signs in the sense that they are reliable indicators of ideas in others' minds or of extra-mental qualities and

[4] See Ayers (1991); for criticism, see Soles (1999).

objects. This epistemic role is clearly differentiated from what I construe as Locke's causal-cum-teleological theory of the representation of simple ideas of sensation.

The second chapter extends Locke's view of signification to so-called "syncategoremata," words such as "if," "and," and "is." I show that Locke's position has the resources to account for the unity of the proposition and propositional attitudes. This chapter provides indirect support for my interpretation, since Locke's view of particles as signs of mental *acts* rather than objects accords well with the claim that words are signals or indicators and poorly with competing conceptions of Locke's linguistic thesis.

Any empiricist account of language as having meaning in virtue of its association with mental objects and acts faces a difficulty in accounting for our ability to talk about kinds of things in addition to particulars. Thus in the third chapter I turn to Locke's account of abstraction, arguing that he conceives of abstraction as mental separation. Locke's somewhat obscure discussion of space, once clarified, in no way conflicts with this reading of abstraction. I defend Locke from some common objections before going on to show how his account of nominal essences functions as a replacement for the Aristotelian view. What is more important, I show how a brand of realism about the (fully particularized) properties of corpuscles and their structures is both implicit in and consistent with Locke's limited form of nominalism. Locke's intriguing strategy is to clearly differentiate the issue of natural kinds and our epistemic access to them from that of universals and properties. This strategy allows him to press his nominalism against the Aristotelians on natural kinds and real essences while retaining a realistic view of properties as particularized natures of the fundamental constituents of the physical world. The latter is necessary, I argue, for grounding Locke's ambitious conception of the laws of nature.

With the rudiments of Locke's view in place, I turn in the fourth chapter to the deployment of his linguistic claims against the Aristotelians. The real essences that the Aristotelians cast as foundational elements in their conception of natural philosophy can be shown, Locke thinks, to be illusory. His argument diagnoses the Aristotelian view as flowing from a misconception of the uses of words. If Locke's view of language is correct, words can at best allow us to unfold our minds to one another; they cannot directly "latch on" to things. A real definition thus becomes a kind of category mistake, since only words can be defined; a real definition, taken as the Aristotelian must intend it to be taken, is simply nonsense. This strand of argument must be seen as independent of the more familiar anti-essentialist arguments.

This argument, I suggest, is an instance of the familiar empiricist "argument from nonsense": rather than showing that a given claim is false, the goal is to show that the words as used by the opposing view are in fact meaningless. In the fifth chapter, I ask whether Locke can lay claim to such arguments without sawing off the branch he sits on. In particular, how can Locke account for meaningful discourse about God, real essence, and substance, given his commitment to seeing all use of language without corresponding ideas in the mind of the speaker as literally nonsensical? In this chapter, I show that Locke's linguistic thesis must be relaxed so as to include ideas in the sense not only of mental objects but of complexes of such objects and mental acts.

In chapter six I briefly discuss the reception of Locke's philosophy of language. I begin by looking at the work of two of Locke's contemporaries (or near-contemporaries), John Sergeant and George Berkeley. Sergeant offers an interesting case of a late-seventeenth-century Aristotelian who wishes to retain his empiricism without falling prey to the "fancies of the ideists." In the course of critiquing Locke's view, Sergeant anticipates many later criticisms.

No account, however brief, of the reception of Locke's writings would be complete without a discussion of Berkeley. Unraveling the tangled skein of Berkeley's arguments allows us to see how the ancient notions of signification both persisted in and were transformed by modern empiricism. I go on to examine criticisms centering around the privacy of the mental: in what sense can two people be said to have the same idea? How can we ever check that they are using the word to signify that idea?

Finally, I draw together the themes of the book by stepping back from the details of Locke's view and examining his overall position on the connection between word and world. This affords an opportunity to consider recent philosophers, such as Hilary Putnam, who see Locke's project of accounting for the intentionality of language in terms of the intentionality of the mental as fundamentally confused. I do not aim for a complete defense of Locke's view, though I do think that these objections are unsuccessful. Rather, my goal is to draw out the content and implications of Locke's view by seeing how it fares in light of some more recent developments.

I have been mindful throughout that some of the topics I discuss, especially abstraction, real essence, and substance, have been the subject of vast heaps of scholarly literature. I have tried to confine myself to those areas on which I felt I had something original to say; where this has not been possible, I have been as brief as clarity permits.

CHAPTER I

Signs and signification

Any discussion of Locke's views on language must begin by explicating his central linguistic notion: signification. This is by no means an easy task, as the sheer variety of available conceptions of signification will attest. Nevertheless, Locke's text clearly commits him to an understanding of signification applicable not only to words but to ideas themselves. Once we unearth this concept, we shall be in a position to come to terms with Locke's arguments for his seemingly counter-intuitive claim that words signify ideas.

WHAT IS LOCKEAN SIGNIFICATION?

Near the start of Book III of *An Essay Concerning Human Understanding*, Locke puts forth what I shall call the "linguistic thesis": "*Words in their primary or immediate Signification, stand for nothing, but the* Ideas *in the Mind of him that uses them*" (III.ii.2: 405). It is helpful to have before us some other statements of the thesis:

The use then of Words, is to be sensible Marks of *Ideas*; and the *Ideas* they stand for, are their proper and immediate Signification. (III.ii.1: 405)

Words, as they are used by Men, can properly and immediately signify nothing but *Ideas*, that are in the Mind of the Speaker . . . (III.ii.4: 406)

[Words'] signification [in a man's use of them] . . . is limited to his *Ideas*, and they can be Signs of nothing else. (III.ii.8: 408)[1]

Obviously, we cannot make a start on interpreting these claims until we know what Locke intends by "signification." The meaning of this word has been fiercely debated, generating interpretations that range from sense and reference to medieval conceptions of signification as making something

---

[1] See also II.xxxi.6: 378: "Names standing for nothing but the *Ideas*, that are in Men's Minds." Also relevant is the "Epistle to the Reader" (1975, p. 13).

known to the intellect. My goal in this chapter is to argue for an admittedly controversial reading of both Locke's thesis and the central argument he offers in support of it.[2]

Many commentators have read Locke's pronouncements above as saying that words *refer* to ideas; that J.S. Mill did so is evident from this famous criticism: "[w]hen I say, 'the sun is the cause of the day,' I do not mean that my idea of the sun causes or excites in me the idea of the day . . ."[3] The semantic idealism produced by reading "signification" in this way is implausible; it could be attractive only to someone antecedently committed to ontological idealism. Much of the scholarship of the past thirty years has been motivated by a desire to defend Locke from this obvious objection. This is clearly one aim of Norman Kretzmann's influential article, "The Main Thesis of Locke's Semantic Theory";[4] it is fair to say that most recent commentators have, with some notable exceptions,[5] followed Kretzmann's reading, at least in its broad outlines. In addition, they have availed themselves (as Kretzmann did not, at least explicitly) of the Fregean distinction between sense and reference. By contrast, E.J. Ashworth has taken issue with such commentators on the grounds that they ignore the context in which Locke was writing. She argues that Locke inherits his conception of signification from the late Scholastics, correctly observing that Locke "does not bother to give a detailed explanation and justification of his claim that words signify ideas primarily and immediately, and this would be a very curious oversight on the part of one who had in mind a doctrine radically different from that normally conveyed by these words."[6] Ashworth is right to say that Locke's arguments in favor of his claim about signification are brief and at best enthymematic. But I shall argue that what the words of the thesis "normally conveyed" can be discovered by looking, not to the

[2] E.J. Lowe briefly offers a similar interpretation of Locke's position in chapter 7 of his (1995).

[3] Mill (1867, p. 15). I am going to call this "Mill's criticism" even though it was anticipated by John Sergeant, a contemporary of Locke's (see below, chapter six). See Sergeant (1984, pp. 33–5). Mill's criticism itself is somewhat unfortunately put, since it depends on reading "is the cause of" in the phrase in question as not itself ideational. To be consistent, Mill's attempted reductio should have it that "is the cause of," or each syntactic element in this phrase, refers to an idea.

[4] Kretzmann (1975).

[5] For example, Charles Landesman claims that Locke sometimes uses "idea" to mean "intentional object" (which at least in some cases is a thing in the world rather than a mental content), and that we can therefore say that words signify ideas, which are (or might be) things in a public environment. "Ideas as immediate significations are things in so far as they are conceived of. Things signified and things immediately signified are the same things" (1976, p. 33). Landesman's account depends on reading Locke as a direct realist, a view I find implausible. Locke's hostility to direct realism is especially evident in a letter to Stillingfleet where Locke argues that the view would entail that the thing thought of actually exists materially in the mind. See Locke (1812, vol. 4, pp. 390–1), discussed below (chapter six). For further argument against reading Locke as a direct realist, see H.E. Matthews (1971).

[6] Ashworth (1981, p. 325).

late Scholastics, but to a tradition whose members include Thomas Hobbes and the authors of the Port-Royal Logic. Before offering my own interpretation, however, I shall explore and argue against those of Kretzmann and Ashworth.

Kretzmann attempts to defend Locke from Mill's criticism by emphasizing the distinction Locke seems to draw between primary and secondary or mediate signification (III.ii.2: 405). Kretzmann writes: "Once it becomes clear that it is only *immediately* that words signify *nothing but* the user's ideas, it is clear also that where the ideas immediately signified are *themselves* signs – that is, are representative ideas – their originals may be *mediately* signified by those words."[7] The force of "immediate" here is this: words immediately signify ideas because it is only in virtue of this connection that they are able to signify things in the world.[8] Because some of these ideas represent real objects or qualities, my ability to refer passes beyond my own mental contents and reaches out to a public realm. As this way of putting matters brings out, Kretzmann seems to be applying the sense/reference distinction to Locke's text; this is how most commentators read Kretzmann.[9] As Kretzmann recognizes, his reading entails that Locke is simply confused when he claims that words and ideas are both signs. (I return to this issue below.)

The major dissenting voice in recent scholarship is that of Ashworth. She suggests that Locke is using the word "signification" in the way late Scholastics such as Burgersdijck used "*significatio*."[10] "*Significatio*" is a technical term that does not mean the same thing as our word "meaning" for a

---

[7] Kretzmann (1975, p. 133).   [8] See Kretzmann (1975, p. 141).

[9] For example, Ashworth (1981, p. 302), says that Kretzmann attempts "to identify the distinction between immediate and mediate signification with the distinction between meaning and reference." The details of how this identification is to be carried out are still very controversial. Consider Stephen Land's treatment of Kretzmann in his (1986, 36ff.). Land writes: "[Kretzmann's] suggested distinction between primary and secondary signification appears to negate the identity of meaning and reference. As a result of this distinction in Lockean theory words may be said to *refer* to ideas in the mind of the speaker but to have *sense* in the public domain beyond their reference." Land suggests that Kretzmann's reading "at least partly" exonerates Locke "from the absurdities of semantic idealism," but I cannot see how this could be, at least on Land's version of Kretzmann. For if ideas are the referents of our words, it is natural to say that we are talking *about* them, about mental contents, and thus Mill's criticism still applies. Further, I find it almost impossible to make sense of this view, as long as sense and reference are given their usual interpretations: sense is supposed to be a "mode of presentation" of an object, while the referent is supposed to be the object itself. See Gottlob Frege, "On Sense and Meaning," in his (1980). Ashworth's reading of Kretzmann, which maps primary signification onto sense and secondary signification onto reference, is both more standard and more plausible. Another recent commentator, Robert Hanna, has taken a different approach in his (1991). On Hanna's view, "intension and extension are equally ideational, for Locke." Thus the only entities fit to serve as primary and secondary significates are ideas. Again, this does not adequately address Mill's criticism.

[10] This is explicit in Ashworth (1984, p. 46): "[P]art of my defense will rest on the claim that Locke was using 'signify' in the same way that his scholastic predecessors used the Latin term '*significare*.'"

variety of reasons;[11] chief among these is that a word's "*significatio* included its reference . . . and seems also to have included elements which belong to meaning rather than reference."[12]

By the early sixteenth century the standard definition of "*significare*" was "to represent some thing or some things or in some way to the cognitive power," where "in some way" was introduced in order to cover the case of such syncategorematic terms as "all" and "none."[13]

Thus the question "what does this word signify?" could be answered correctly "by a statement about the term's total denotation."[14] Locke, according to Ashworth, adopted the view held by for example Burgersdijck, whereby one can say that "concepts are signified, since it is by means of concepts that things are signified, and the means of signifying must itself be signified."[15] Thus "signification" encompasses, for Locke as well as the Scholastics, such things as making known, expressing, and revealing, and it involves aspects of both sense and reference.[16]

Ashworth and Kretzmann represent the two main schools of thought on this issue. In my view, both are off the mark. We can begin to see that something has gone wrong in each of their views by examining the arguments they attribute to Locke.

Near the start of Book III, Locke argues that since one cannot immediately disclose to another the contents of his mind, one must "be *able to use these* [articulate] *Sounds, as Signs of internal Conceptions*; and to make them stand as marks for the *Ideas* within his own Mind, whereby they might be made known to others . . . " (III.i.2: 402).[17] Very similar arguments appear in the Port-Royal *Logic*[18] and Hobbes's *De Corpore*.[19] Kretzmann[20] and

---

[11] For a detailed list and evaluation of these reasons, see Michael Losonsky (1994, p. 128ff.).

[12] Ashworth (1981, p. 310).   [13] Ashworth (1984, p. 60); see also (1981, p. 310).

[14] Ashworth (1984, p. 61).   [15] Ashworth (1981, p. 324).

[16] Ashworth (1981, pp. 309–11). For another discussion and critique of Ashworth's view, see Michael Losonsky's (1994).

[17] This same point recurs in the next chapter: "The Comfort, and Advantage of Society, not being to be had without Communication of Thoughts, it was necessary, that Man should find out some external sensible Signs, whereby those invisible *Ideas*, which his thoughts are made up of, might be made known to others" (III.ii.1: 405, also quoted in Ashworth (1981, p. 313)). See also II.xi.9: 159: "The use of Words then being to stand as outward Marks of our internal *Ideas*," as well as Locke's "Epistle to the Reader" (1975, p. 13).

[18] Arnauld and Nicole (1970, p. 78). The authors there speak of "our need to use external signs to make ourselves understood . . ." My translations usually follow those of Jill Vance Buroker (Arnauld and Nicole 1996).

[19] See *De Corpore* I.ii.3 (Hobbes 1839–45, vol. 1, p. 15); compare Hobbes (1994, p. 39): "And men desiring to shew others the knowledge, opinions, conceptions, and passions which are within themselves, and to that end having invented language . . ."

[20] See Kretzmann (1975, p. 127ff.).

Ashworth[21] agree that this "argument from the uses of words" establishes (at most) that words used in communication are signs of ideas. It leaves open that words might be signs of something else as well and so does not adequately support the thesis insofar as the thesis involves the claim that words (immediately) signify *nothing but* ideas.

How, then, is the thesis to be supported? On this question there is, surprisingly enough, something like a consensus.[22] According to Kretzmann, Locke attempts to establish the thesis with "the argument from the doctrine of representative ideas."[23] This argument is worth examining in some detail.

Kretzmann purports to find the argument in this passage:

Nor can anyone apply them [words], as Marks, immediately to anything else, but the *Ideas*, that he himself hath: For this would be to make them Signs of his own Conceptions, and yet apply them to other *Ideas*; which would be to make them Signs, and not Signs of his *Ideas* at the same time; and so in effect, to have no Signification at all. (III.ii.2: 405)

On Kretzmann's view, the argument attempts to show that the only things one can immediately signify with words are one's ideas and is thus designed to bolster precisely the aspect of the thesis left unsupported by the argument from the uses of words. Locke's argument is supposed to be this: since any successful use of x to immediately signify y (where y is not an idea of mine) presupposes that I have an idea of y, to say that x could immediately signify y would be to say that I could use x to signify y without having an idea of y, which is impossible.[24] Kretzmann sees a strong connection between Locke's epistemological and semantic views: it is because representationalism – the view that we know the world only through the mediation of ideas – is true that we cannot succeed in referring to an object unless we have an idea of it that is itself a sign in the sense that it represents that object.[25]

---

[21] This corresponds to the second of the four arguments she finds in Smiglecius, three of which she attributes to Locke in her (1981, p. 312 ff.). See below, n. 26.

[22] For Ashworth, see her (1981, p. 317) (quoted below). I find her agreement with Kretzmann here puzzling, since, if Locke meant by "signify" something as different from what Kretzmann takes him to mean by that term as Ashworth supposes, one would expect the arguments in favor of the thesis that crucially involve that term to be correspondingly different from the arguments Kretzmann gives.

[23] Kretzmann (1975, p. 130).

[24] See Kretzmann (1975, pp. 132–3): "[M]y applying (or attempting to apply) a word to signify something other than an idea of mine presupposes that I have an idea of that thing associated with that word. If I had no idea of that thing I could not make it the object of my attention or any action of mine. Thus, whenever I genuinely use . . . a word . . . that utterance of mine signifies *immediately* some idea of mine, whatever other meaning I may give or think I give to the word. Therefore, if X is something other than an idea of mine, to suppose that I can apply a word to signify X *immediately* is to suppose that I can apply a word to signify X while I have no idea of X, which is impossible."

[25] Ashworth (1981, p. 325) writes, "I think that Kretzmann was right when he mentioned Locke's representative theory of perception in the context of his theory of language. If ideas are the immediate

Ashworth attributes to Locke three arguments that she also finds in late scholastic writings.[26] One of these is "very closely related, if not identical to . . . the argument from representative ideas"[27] we have just been discussing. Here Locke takes over an argument from Smiglecius: since "things could not be signified by words unless by virtue of the concept (*ratio*) by which they were conceived," "concepts are immediately signified."[28] The inference pattern is the same: that ideas/concepts are immediately signified by words is to be supported by the claim that they are indispensable to signification.

But something is amiss in this dominant account of Locke's reasoning. In fact, the argument is fallacious. Even if it establishes that ideas are a necessary condition of the meaningful use of language, how does it follow from this that ideas are themselves what is signified?[29] The fact that x is a necessary condition for signification in no way tends to show that x is what is signified, whether primarily or in some other way.

Consider Kretzmann's statement of the argument. The position that has to be ruled out here is that words signify or immediately signify ideas *and* something else, viz., extra-mental things. But in order to show that there's a difficulty with this position, Kretzmann has to build into the opposing view the claim that the speaker lacks an idea of the thing she (immediately) signifies, and this is to beg the question. Kretzmann might also be assuming that a word can only signify or immediately signify one thing at a time. But again, this begs the question. Surely Locke's opponent need not claim that in (immediately) signifying x she lacks an idea of x. More important, she might grant that having an idea of x is a necessary condition for signifying x and still deny that the idea is the thing signified, whether immediately or otherwise.

Ashworth's statement of the argument is in the same position. In fact, Smiglecius himself, in the very text she supposes Locke to be drawing from,

---

objects of perception, then it makes good sense that they should also be the immediate objects of signification."

[26] Ashworth lays out four arguments she finds in scholastic sources, especially Smiglecius: the first is an appeal to the authority of Aristotle; the second, the argument from the uses of words; the third, an argument from the premise that one who conceives nothing signifies nothing (which I address below); and fourth, an inference from the premise that words can only signify things by means of concepts. She says that "each one of them, apart from the appeal to Aristotle, is found in Locke's chapter on the signification of words" (Ashworth, 1984, p. 62). See also (1981, p. 312ff.).

[27] Ashworth (1981, p. 317).   [28] Ashworth (1981, p. 316).

[29] Ashworth in effect makes this point when she criticizes the argument from representative ideas by saying, "the move from the premise that ideas are necessary for the significant use of language to the conclusion that ideas are what is signified has been left unjustified" (1981, p. 302). She gives the impression there that the later portion of her article will improve upon Kretzmann's reading of Locke's argument; but this promise is never fulfilled.

goes on to point out the fallacy. Ashworth is aware of this, but seems not to find it implausible that Locke would lift a straightforwardly fallacious argument from one of the very figures he wishes to attack.

The same problem infects another argument Ashworth attributes to Locke,[30] which is based on the premise that those who lack the relevant concepts do not succeed in signifying anything by their words; that is, their utterances are mere parrot-talk (see III.ii.7: 408). But again, there is no legitimate inference from the fact that x is a necessary condition for signification to the conclusion that x is what is signified.

We have now exhausted the two most important attempts to interpret Locke's thesis and his arguments for it. We have also found good reason to be dissatisfied with them. Yet the fact that an argument is obviously fallacious is no reason, by itself, to hold off from attributing that argument to a great dead philosopher. I shall argue, however, that the interpretation I present below not only secures for Locke a valid argument for his thesis without committing him to semantic idealism, but is better grounded in the text.

TWO SEMIOTIC TRADITIONS

Ashworth is right in thinking that we must look at the larger context in which Locke was writing. But which one? Writings of the modern period and earlier offer a wide variety of notions of sign. We can make some progress by exploring other such notions that were available to Locke in texts we know he read.

I want to argue that a plausible source of inspiration for Locke's views has been staring us in the face. We must look, not to the Aristotelians, but to writers with whom Locke had much more sympathy, such as Hobbes and the Port-Royalians.

Consider Hobbes's discussion of signification in his *De Corpore* (1655), published some thirty-four years before the *Essay*. There, Hobbes writes,

Now, those things we call SIGNS are the *antecedents of their consequents, and the consequents of their antecedents, as often as we observe them to go before or follow after in the same manner.* For example, a thick cloud is a sign of rain to follow, and rain a sign that a cloud has gone before, for this reason only, that we seldom see clouds without the consequence of rain, nor rain at any time but when a cloud has gone before. And of signs, some are *natural*, whereof I have already given an example, others are *arbitrary*, namely, those we make choice of at our own pleasure, as a bush

---

[30] This is the third argument listed above in n. 26.

hung up, signifies that wine is to be sold there; a stone set in the ground signifies the bound of a field; and words so and so connected, signify the cogitations and motions of our mind. (*De Corpore* I.ii.2)[31]

We might say that signification in Hobbes's sense amounts to indication: rain indicates the recent presence of a cloud; a bush, the presence of wine-selling. As Hobbes's examples make clear, the notion is not an essentially causal one: a bush does not cause wine-selling.[32] It is also neutral with regard to temporal sequence: ashes can signify a fire, and a dark cloud can signify rain. (Indeed, there may be no temporal sequence at all, as in the bush example.) Etymologically, the notion survives in our word "signaling."[33] This notion of signification is distinct from those suggested by Kretzmann and Ashworth. Clearly, it does not map onto sense, reference, or any mixture of both: a rain cloud or a bush outside a wine shop is not the right sort of thing to have a *Sinn* or a *Bedeutung*.[34] Neither is it Ashworth's "making known": every act of indicating x might also be an act of making x known (or revealing or expressing x), but the converse is clearly false.

It is not obvious what Hobbes means by calling sign and thing signified (or, as I shall call it, significate) antecedent and consequent. His discussion makes sense only when located in a tradition whose chief members include Aristotle, the Stoics, Sextus Empiricus, and, in the modern period, Pierre Gassendi. This tradition, as we shall see, is deeply at odds with that of the late Scholastics.

In the *Prior Analytics*, Aristotle says that a sign is *protasis apodeiktike e anankia e endoxos* (70a6–7), "a proposition, either necessary or reputable, used to show something."[35] Signs, then, have a role in inference; sign-inferences are enthymematic arguments on Aristotle's view (see *Prior Analytics* 70a10 and *Rhetoric* 1355a6). Signs play the role of antecedents in

---

[31] Hobbes (1839–45, vol. 1, pp. 14–15).

[32] This is not to say, of course, that apprehending a sign cannot cause knowledge of the thing signified. The point is that there is not necessarily any causal connection *between* x and y, where x is a sign of y, or vice versa.

[33] This kind of signification has a parallel in H.P. Grice's notion of "natural meaning"; see Grice (1957). He uses the following examples to explicate this notion: "Those spots mean (meant) measles"; "the recent budget means that we shall have a hard year" (1957, p. 377). Grice, of course, does not identify linguistic meaning with natural meaning.

[34] Ian Hacking makes a similar point in his (1975b, p. 22).

[35] The translation is Burnyeat's; see his (1982, p. 198). Aristotle also says, "[A]nything such that when it is another thing is, or when it has come into being the other has come into being before or after, is a sign of the other's being or having come into being" (*Prior Analytics* 70a8–10, in Aristotle 1984, vol. 1, p. 112). This omits the epistemic considerations common to most other definitions of "sign." But I take it that the characterization of signs given in the text above remedies this by bringing out the role signs have in inference.

conditional claims: to use one of Aristotle's examples, if this woman is lactating (sign), then she has recently given birth (significate). It is at first sight odd to see signs defined as propositions. In Aristotle's examples, they are states of affairs or facts. But as M.F. Burnyeat[36] points out, both ordinary Greek and ordinary English allow us to say "X is a sign of . . ." and "*that p* is a sign of . . ." interchangeably.[37]

A necessary sign is an evidence (*tekmerion*), while a reputable sign "has no specific name" (*Rhetoric* 1357b3–5). A reputable sign figures in a refutable deduction; so if we infer that the wise are just from the fact that Socrates is wise and just, "we certainly have a sign, but even though the proposition is true, the argument is refutable, since it does not form a deduction" (*Rhetoric* 1357b13–14). The fact that Socrates is wise and just does not make it necessary that all other wise men should be just; this inference is an invalid third-figure syllogism. Similarly, the sign-inference from the fact that this woman is pale to the conclusion that she is pregnant is an invalid second-figure syllogism.[38] These arguments are always refutable, even if true (*Rhetoric* 1357b17–21). By contrast, if one infers from the fact that a woman is lactating that she has recently given birth, one has got hold of a necessary truth, and so the basis for inference is an evidence or *tekmerion*.[39]

One difficulty in Aristotle's account is that reputable sign-inferences are invalid.[40] Aristotle says that "[t]ruth may be found in signs of whatever kind" (*Prior Analytics* 70a37–8),[41] but this seems cold comfort, since of course any fallacious argument may have true premises and a true conclusion. The source of the difficulty, perhaps, is that syllogistic logic is rather a Procrustean bed for sign-inferences.[42] But it seems clear that Aristotle is not suggesting that merely reputable signs and the arguments in which

---

[36] Burnyeat (1982, p. 198).
[37] The same issue recurs with the Stoics, who, as we shall see, say that sign is a proposition that forms the antecedent of a sound conditional. On their account, a proposition is a *lekton* that is incorporeal and so cannot, strictly speaking, be said to exist (see Long and Sedley 1987, vol. 1, pp. 195–201). The same line of thought Burnyeat offers in the case of Aristotle can also be offered here.
[38] Alternatively, one might say that it is an instance of affirming the consequent: if *x* is pregnant, *x* is pale; *a* is a pale woman; therefore *a* is pregnant. Philodemus would treat a woman's pallor as a "common" sign, which can exist whether or not its significate does, as opposed to the "particular" sign, which exists only when its significate does (see *de Signis* XIV, in Philodemus 1941, p. 55).
[39] Of course, as Burnyeat points out, this is not in fact an instance of a necessary truth.
[40] See *Prior Analytics* 70a28–37.
[41] Aristotle seems to be using "*semeia*" here to refer to arguments based on signs. For the different uses of this term in Aristotle, see H. Weidemann (1989).
[42] Alternatively, one might suggest that the problem is simply that Aristotle lacks the proper operators, such as "probably," "generally," and so on.

they figure be dismissed as worthless. Instead, he seems to be insisting that there are logically invalid inferences that are nevertheless of value.

The Stoics take a harder line, arguing that only *tekmeria* are signs. On their account, a sign is the antecedent proposition "in a sound conditional, revelatory of the consequent."[43] We can cast the sign-inference from, say, motion to the existence of the void thus: if there is motion, then there is void. Thus *there is motion* is revelatory of its consequent just because it could not be true unless there were also void. It is crucial that not just any conditional, but only a sound one, will do; the question is, what is the criterion for soundness? On this point there does not seem to have been agreement. Sextus attributes to an early Stoic, Philo, the view that a sound conditional is any conditional except one with a true antecedent and a false consequent. But later Stoics such as Chrysippus introduced the criterion of *sunartesis* or cohesion, according to which a conditional is sound just in case the denial of the consequent conflicts with its antecedent.[44] The test of the soundness of a conditional is *anaskeue*, the "elimination method": in thinking away the consequent, does one *thereby* think away the antecedent? It is tempting to render *anaskeue* as contraposition, but this would be inadequate, as even a Philonian material conditional, if true, would live up to it. Here is an example that passes the one test but not the other: "If I am typing, it is night." Both propositions happen now to be true. But in denying the consequent, I do not thereby deny or think away the antecedent. They simply lack the proper connection.[45]

Sextus Empiricus draws a distinction between kinds of sign that will be of crucial importance not only for our understanding of Locke, but of Berkeley as well (see chapter six). Sextus adds to the Stoic definition of sign an epistemic component: for his purposes, he defines an "indicative sign" as a sign whose significate is not itself observable. This he wishes to distinguish from a reminiscent or commemorative sign, which is not a basis for inference. In an influential passage, Sextus claims that "the dogmatists" hold that

---

[43] Long and Sedley (1987, vol. 1, p. 209).

[44] Sextus Empiricus, *Outlines of Pyrrhonism* 2.110–13, in Long and Sedley (1987, vol. 1, p. 209).

[45] Here it is instructive to compare the way in which the material conditional fails to capture coun- terfactuals. For an extended argument against rendering *anaskeue* as "contraposition," see David Sedley's (1982, p. 245). Sedley traces *anaskeue* to *anarein* as it figures in Aristotle's *Categories*. There Aristotle discusses pairs of terms such as half/double, slave/master, which are such that eliminat- ing the one thereby eliminates the other. Such terms are relatives, in Aristotle's terminology. It is then the meanings of the terms involved that allow some conditionals to pass the elimination test.

[t]hose [matters] which are occasionally non-evident and those that are by nature non-evident are grasped by means of signs, but the former by means of reminiscent signs (*hypomnêstika*) and the latter by means of indicative signs (*endeiktika*) . . . They call a reminiscent sign that which, having been observed together with [the occasionally non-evident thing] that it is a sign of, is, because of its being evident to someone at the time it occurs, a reminder to us of that which it was observed together with, though the latter is non-evident; for example, as in the case of smoke and fire. An indicative sign, they say, is that which is not evidently observable together with that which it is a sign of, but, as a result of its own peculiar nature and constitution, signifies that of which it is a sign, as, for example, the motions of the body are signs of the soul. Hence they define this [kind of] sign thus: "an indicative sign is the antecedent proposition in a sound conditional revelatory of the consequent."[46]

A "reminiscent" or "empirical" sign signifies something we have previously experienced; it brings to mind its significate in virtue of past association. An "indicative" sign, on the other hand, signifies something hidden. "The hidden" here means that which is imperceptible but knowable by inference. Commenting on this passage from Sextus, Gassendi says that an indicative sign signifies that which is naturally hidden "because it is of such a nature that it could not exist unless the thing exists, and therefore whenever it exists, the thing also exists."[47] Gassendi's favorite example (drawn from Aristotle) is invisible pores in the skin: sweating is an indicative sign of these pores just because one could not sweat unless such pores were present. Using this distinction, Sextus is able to distinguish his position from that of the dogmatists: he is arguing only against indicative signs, not reminiscent ones. For the latter are not grounds for inference; they carry no justificatory weight.[48]

The distinction between signs-as-reminders and signs-as-indicators is also to be found in Augustine and in Hobbes. Augustine argues that "we don't learn anything by these signs called words"; at best, "they remind us to look for things."[49] This is contrary to the naïve view that there is in

---

[46] *Outlines of Pyrrhonism* 2.97–2.101, in Inwood and Gerson (1988, p. 214).

[47] Gassendi (1972, p. 332).

[48] "[W]e are not arguing against every sign, but only against the indicative sign, on the grounds that it seems to have been concocted by the dogmatists. For the reminiscent sign has been found to be trustworthy by everyday life, since when someone sees smoke, he takes it as a sign of fire, and seeing a scar he says that there has been a wound. Hence, not only are we not in conflict with everyday life, but we are even allied with it, by assenting undogmatically to that which has been made trustworthy by it, while opposing only those which have been especially invented by the dogmatists." *Outlines of Pyrrhonism* 2.102, in Inwood and Gerson (1988, p. 215).

[49] *De magistro* in Augustine (1995, p. 137).

fact some content being transmitted with or through the words.[50] A sign merely "brings something else to the mind."[51] But Adeodatus, Augustine's interlocutor in *de magistro*, eventually compels Augustine to admit, however grudgingly, that "when words are heard by someone who knows them, he can know that the speaker had been thinking about the things they signify."[52] In this sense they not only bring something else to mind, they serve as a means of knowing what another speaker is thinking about.

Hobbes deploys the same distinction with regard to words, this time drawing it between *marks* and *signs*. Hobbes writes,

> [T]he first use of names, is to serve for *marks*, or *notes* of remembrance. Another is, when many use the same words, to signify, by their connexion and order, one to another, what they conceive, or think of each matter; and also what they desire, fear, or have any other passion for. And for this use they are called *signs*.[53]

A speaker or writer can use words to remind himself of thoughts he had previously. Their use in this capacity is purely private; that is, they are marks only for the person who writes or speaks them. In their second use, as signs, they allow others to infer what is present in the mind of the speaker.

It is worth pointing out that in antiquity, the debate over signs was primarily epistemological, with linguistic considerations usually coming in as an after-thought. (Augustine is the obvious exception here.) This might help to explain why some philosophers, such as the Stoics, claim that the connection between sign and significate must be necessary. Had they considered words as signs, they might have been brought to admit that some indicators can stand in a contingent relation to what they indicate and still serve their purpose.

However that may be, I now wish to draw attention to what all of these figures have in common: the belief that a sign must be available as an object of sensation. Augustine's statement of this point is clearest: a sign is "something which is itself sensed and which indicates to the mind something beyond the sign itself."[54] There is a competing tradition that has its source in the late Scholastic period. Ashworth is correct in saying that by the early sixteenth century the standard meaning of "*significare*" was "to represent some thing or some things or in some way to the cognitive power." But this

---

[50] For his description of the opposed position, see his *Homilies on John the Evangelist* 37.4.14–24, quoted in Augustine (1995, p. xvi).

[51] *De doctrina Christiana* II.i.1, in Augustine (1958, p. 27).

[52] *De magistro* 13.45, in Augustine (1995, p. 145).

[53] *Leviathan* I.4, in Hobbes (1839–45, vol. 3, pp. 19–20).

[54] *De Dialectica* v, in Augustine (1975, p. 87). See also *de Doctrina Christiana* I.ii.2 and *de Trinitate* XV.xi.20. A helpful discussion is to be found in R.A. Markus (1957).

is a revision of the notion of sign common to the Augustinian tradition. The latter was thought by the late Scholastics to be too narrow to accommodate concepts or acts of knowing, which the late scholastics wanted to call "formal signs." John Poinsot (a.k.a. John of St. Thomas, 1589–1644) writes that a formal sign is "the formal awareness which represents of itself";[55] a formal sign is not, in the first instance, an object of thought, but that *by which* thought is accomplished. A reflexive act is required to bring the formal sign to consciousness. In the latter half of the sixteenth century, the Conimbricenses, a group of commentators on Aristotle centered in Coimbra, Spain, explicitly rejected Augustine's definition on the grounds that it ruled out formal signs.[56] This rejection of the Augustinian definition was, in the words of Ashworth, a "mere commonplace by the beginning of the sixteenth century."[57] Augustine, it was claimed, had only defined "instrumental" signs. The notion of formal signs, signs that do not themselves have to be perceived, survives in the modern period in the works of Descartes, Glanvill, and the Cambridge Platonists.[58]

To avoid confusion, I wish to impose a technical vocabulary on this spectrum of views. I shall call an *indicative* sign any sign whose significate is of necessity unavailable to perception, and which serves as an indication of that significate. I depart from the Hellenistic tradition in leaving open the question of necessary connection. A *reminiscent* sign is one whose presence conveys the mind by a causal process to something else which has been experienced in conjunction with that sign. There is room for confusion here, since we often say, even in the case of indicative signs, that we have been caused or made to think of something or that something is the case. It is as natural to say that sweat brings about the thought of pores in the skin as that smoke brings about the thought of fire. The relevant distinction is that reminiscent signs depend on prior experience of constant conjunctions, experience which is by definition unavailable in the case of indicative signs. Reminiscent signification is perhaps best understood as

---

[55] *Tractatus de Signis*, in Poinsot (1995, p. 27). See John P. Doyle's (1984) and Ashworth (1990, p. 39). There, Ashworth writes, "[f]or something to signify formally was [according to Soto] simply for it to be a concept or an act of knowing."

[56] *Commentarii Conimbricenses in dialecticam Aristotelis* (1607, 6, q.1, a.1), quoted in Doyle (1984, p. 569). A formal sign is contrasted with an instrumental sign, which, in the words of John Poinsot, "represents something other than itself from a pre-existing cognition of itself as an object, as the footprint of an ox represents an ox" (Doyle, 1984, p. 27). His definition of sign in general is "[t]hat which represents something other than itself to a cognitive power" (Doyle, 1984, p. 25); in this, he follows Domingo de Soto. According to Soto, Augustine had merely defined an instrumental sign. See Ashworth (1988, esp. pp. 138–9).

[57] Ashworth, (1988, p. 138).   [58] See Yolton (1984) and (2000).

expectation; whether this expectation is justified is another question I wish
to leave open.

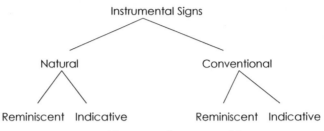

Figure 1: Taxonomy of Instrumental Signs

A further set of useful distinctions is to be found in the Port-Royal *Logic*.[59]
Arnauld and Nicole discuss both conventional and natural indicative signs;
as examples of the latter, they offer the expression of a face as a sign of a
mental attitude and warm ashes as the sign of a fire; as examples of the
former, they cite words as conventional signs of thoughts.[60]

Their classifications cut across the categories of reminiscent and indicative signs, even if some of the sub-categories so constructed are empty. The
most obvious distinction, already discussed, is (a) that between natural and
conventional signs. Natural signs do not depend on human activity; conventional signs are arbitrary.[61] The next (b) is drawn between signs whose
significates are copresent with them, and those whose significates are not.[62]
One difference between the way in which warm ashes are a sign of fire
and rain is a sign of a cloud is that the fire temporally precedes the ashes,
while rainfall and a cloud are copresent. Arnauld and Nicole also distinguish between (c) signs whose presence ensures the existence of the thing
signified – "as respiration is a sign of the life of animals"[63] – and signs from
whose presence we can only conclude the *probable* existence of the thing
signified – as "pallor is only a probable sign of pregnancy in women."[64]

---

[59] We can be fairly certain that Locke was familiar with the Port-Royal Logic, as Harrison and Laslett
list both French and Latin editions of *La Logique* as present in Locke's library. See their (1971, p. 75).
Harrison and Laslett do not list a copy of Hobbes's *De Corpore* as among his possessions; however,
he did have a copy of *Leviathan*, among other of Hobbes's works.

[60] "[L]es mots sont signes d'institution des pensées," Arnauld and Nicole (1970, p. 82). And later: "On
peut dire en général sur ce sujet, que les mots sont des sons distincts & articulés, dont les hommes
ont fait des signes pour marquer ce qui se passe dans leur esprit" (1970, p. 143).

[61] (1970, p. 82).   [62] (1970, p. 81).

[63] "[C]omme la respiration l'est de la vie des animaux" (1970, p. 80).

[64] "[L]a pâleur n'est qu'un signe probable de grossesse dans les femmes" (1970, p. 80).

As we have seen, this distinction was captured by the tradition as holding between those signs which are "necessary" and those which are merely "probable."[65]

If a given sign is conventional, we can safely infer several of its other features. First, in order for a conventional signification relation to be set up, the parties concerned must have perceptual access to the signifier. No conventional sign, it seems, could be a formal sign. Consider Hobbes's example (itself borrowed from the traditional logicians) of the bush in front of the wine shop: my wine business will hardly be improved by signifying that I sell wine by some sign of which no one could be aware. A bush outside the shop is useful precisely because perceptual access to it is (at least pre-theoretically) unproblematic. It is an open question, as yet, what kind of access (if any) we must have to the thing signified. Thus, it seems fair to say that any conventional sign will have to be instrumental rather than formal. Adherence to the Augustinian tradition on this point seems mandatory. With regard to (b), conventional signification is indifferent. With regard to (c), however, it seems clear that the relation is merely probable. We can easily imagine conventions such that in one context, x signifies y, while in another, x signifies z.

We are now in a position to return to Locke.

IDEAS AS SIGNS

How, then, does Locke understand signification? Which of these competing traditions best captures the sense of the term in his mouth?

A natural place to begin is Locke's discussion of ideas, which he also calls signs.[66] As we have seen, Kretzmann is driven to claim that Locke equivocates when he calls both ideas and words "signs."[67] A reading that is able to account for his use of this term in both ideational and linguistic contexts naturally has the advantage.

Locke argues that our simple ideas "agree to the reality of things" whether or not they resemble anything in the external world. For they are "designed to be the Marks, whereby we are to know, and distinguish Things, which we have to do with" (II.xxx.2: 372–3). Whether they are "only constant Effects,

---

[65] See Gassendi's *Syntagma* Part I in Gassendi (1972, p. 330). Gassendi refers to Aristotle's *Rhetoric* 1357b and the *Prior Analytics* II.xxvii, as well as to Quintilian, *Institutio oratoria* V, ix. Aristotle says that signs that are merely probable indicators of their significates lack a name; Quintilian provides one, saying that "the Greeks" called those signs which are "necessary" *tekmêria*, and those which are not *sêmeia*.

[66] " . . . [T]here are two sorts of Signs commonly made use of, *viz. Ideas* and *Words*" (IV.v.2: 574).

[67] Kretzmann (1975, p. 135).

or else exact Resemblances of something in the things themselves," such ideas are dependable marks or signs[68] of the objects or qualities of objects that can cause us to have those ideas. Ideas of sensation serve as grounds for inference to their causes: when I have a piece of paper before me in certain conditions, the idea *white* is produced in my mind, "by which I know, that that Quality or Accident (*i.e.* whose appearance before my Eyes, always causes that *Idea*) doth really exist" (IV.xi.2: 631). In this case, my having the idea *white* gives me a basis for inference to the presence of a secondary quality in a physical object.[69] It is in this sense that the idea is a sign or mark of its cause.

Consider Locke's response to the inverted spectrum problem. We have seen that an idea of sensation is a sign of its cause. Locke uses this premise to argue that it would not "carry any Imputation of *Falshood* to our simple *Ideas, if* by the different Structure of our Organs, it were so ordered, That *the same Object should produce in several Men's Minds* [qualitatively] *different* Ideas at the same time" (II.xxxii.15: 389).[70] What matters about the idea we connect with "blue" is not its qualitative content, but rather its epistemic role. That the same object should produce in us qualitatively different ideas in no way undermines our claim to have the same ideas, because the criteria of sameness here are not qualitative.[71] Instead, Locke appeals to what we might call *significative* sameness, sameness of idea *qua* sign. Two ideas of a secondary quality are the same, on this view, if they are evidence for the presence of the same extra-mental object or quality that causes them.[72]

Ideas of sensation are thus indicative instrumental signs that allow us to infer to the objects and qualities that cause them, which are necessarily hidden from us. But how do ideas come to represent their objects in the first place? Unsurprisingly, the causal connection that funds indicative sign inferences in the case of simple ideas also accounts for their role as representations. The epistemic function of ideas presupposes a distinct means of

---

[68] Note that unlike Hobbes Locke uses the terms "mark" and "sign" interchangeably. For example, immediately after stating that words signify ideas in III.ii, Locke writes, "That then which Words are the Marks of, are the *Ideas* of the Speaker: Nor can any one apply them, as Marks, immediately to anything else, but the *Ideas*, he himself hath" (III.ii.2: 405).

[69] On this issue, see Michael Ayers (1998b, pp. 24–47) and (1991, vol. 1, *passim*).

[70] We must be careful to distinguish different criteria for the sameness of ideas. For if numerical identity is at issue, it is obvious that the same object must produce different ideas in distinct minds. The sentence immediately following the one quoted in the text makes clear that qualitative difference is what is meant here.

[71] Nevertheless, given our common physical makeup, Locke is "very apt to think, that the sensible *Ideas*, produced by any Object in different Men's Minds, are most commonly very near and undiscernibly alike" (II.xxxii.15: 389). But by Locke's lights, this is a side issue to be settled by physiology rather than philosophy.

[72] For a related treatment of the inverted spectrum issue, see Michael Losonsky (1994).

representing what is indicated; causal co-variance provides this means, even if, as we shall see, Locke supplements this with teleological considerations.

Locke argues that simple ideas "represent to us Things under those appearances which they are fitted to produce in us: whereby we are enabled to distinguish the sorts of particular Substances, to discern the states they are in, and so to take them for our Necessities, and apply them to our Uses" (IV.iv.4: 564). This and many other passages suggest that Locke is offering a causal account of representation familiar from the work of Jerry Fodor.[73] We must note, however, that Locke applies his causal account only to *simple* ideas; his distinct treatment of the representation of complex ideas will be treated below (chapter three). What is more important, Locke's causal account contains a teleological element.

A causal account on its own runs into two serious problems. First, it is unclear how a simple idea could ever *mis*represent anything. If idea x represents quality or thing y just in case y causes x, then, by the very nature of the case, there is no sense to be made of an x that misrepresents its y. A closely related problem is that of disjunction: if an idea of green, for example, is caused sometimes by green things and sometimes by red things, what it represents is no longer the quality green but the disjunction of green and red. It is typical for causal theorists to appeal to standard conditions to solve these problems: a properly functioning cognitive system in standard conditions will token *green* only in response to things genuinely having that quality. However tempting this move might seem, Robert Cummins has argued that it is impossible to specify these standard conditions in a non-circular way.[74]

Locke never explicitly addresses these problems. His account has the resources to do so, however.[75] For Locke is not simply a causal theorist: his account includes a teleological element, built on God's role in setting up the relation of causation between simple ideas and things. He need not appeal to standard conditions on their own because the disjunction and misrepresentation problems can be solved by appeal to design: "God in his Wisdom, having set [simple ideas] as Marks of Distinction in Things, whereby we may be able to discern one Thing from another; and so chuse any of them for our uses, as we have Occasion" (II.xxxii.14: 388). A tokening of an idea is veridical just in case it is caused by the quality or object that God intended. Alternatively, we can say that veridical tokenings are those that take place under normal conditions. "Normal conditions" must,

---

[73] See Fodor (1987).   [74] See Cummins (1989, p. 46).
[75] My thoughts here are very much in line with those of Sally Ferguson's (2001).

of course, be cashed out in non-intentional terms. The appeal to teleology allows precisely this: normal conditions are just those under which ideas function as they are supposed to, that is, as indications of the relevant extra-mental object or quality.

Contemporary naturalists have replaced divine teleology with that of natural selection. The result is the same: misrepresentation can be accounted for in terms of the purposes of God (or the *ersatz* purposes of natural selection) in setting up the connection between objects and mental representations. The disjunction problem also disappears once we see that the reference of a mental representation is fixed by the purposes of the creator. As Sally Ferguson puts it, "the intentionality of the designer trickles down to the thing designed."[76]

These issues will become important again when we consider Locke's doctrine of abstraction (chapter 3), and in applying his linguistic views to his official definition of knowledge and his replies to skepticism (chapter seven). For now, it is enough to note that the role of ideas as indicative signs is distinct from their role as representations, even though the same relation, causation, underlies both.

WORDS AS SIGNS

I have been arguing that in his epistemology Locke exploits a notion of sign as an indication or an evidence, a grounds for inference. Given this, the most natural interpretation of Locke's claim that *words* are signs of ideas in the mind of the speaker is that words serve as indicators or signals of those ideas. Consider once again Locke's argument from the uses of words. A person's thoughts "are all within his own Breast, invisible, and hidden from others, nor can of themselves be made to appear" (III.ii.1: 405). The use of words lies in their capacity "to stand as outward Marks of our internal *Ideas*" (II.xi.9: 159). The case is exactly parallel with that of ideas of sensation: they, too, must serve as signs of what is hidden, since only our ideas (and perhaps our own minds)[77] are immediately present to us. Note that the signification relation in the case of ideas of sensation is dependent on causation; it is the fact that an idea of blue, for instance, is caused by an object with the proper secondary quality that allows the idea to serve as a sign of that quality. To say that words are conventional signs is just to say that the signification relation in their case is dependent upon

---

[76] Ferguson (2001, p. 118).

[77] For the suggestion that our own minds might be immediately present to us, see IV.xxi.4: 720–1.

their role in an artificial, shared convention rather than in a natural relation such as causation.

Although Locke's focus is usually on words as instruments of communication, and so as indicative signs, he nevertheless follows the spirit (but not the letter) of Hobbes's distinction between signs and marks. Immediately before stating the linguistic thesis in III.ii.2, Locke writes,

The use Men have of these Marks [i.e., words], being either to record their own Thoughts for the Assistance of their own Memory; or as it were, to bring out their *Ideas*, and lay them before the view of others: *Words in their primary or immediate Signification, stand for nothing, but the* Ideas *in the Mind of him that uses them* . . . (III.ii.2: 405)

Note that this statement of the thesis declares not just that words are signs of ideas in the mind of the speaker, as is usually the case, but more broadly, in the mind of the person making use of the words. This allows for words to serve as Hobbesian marks, a use I take to involve, at least paradigmatically, writing rather than speech. One might jot down words for her own use and come back to them later, so as to remind herself of what she had been thinking, or one might use them as signs to others of her ideas. In either case, they are signs only of the user's ideas.

It is important to see that Locke's philosophy of language is partly normative. His claim is that the purpose of speech is to allow us to offer each other sensible signs of our ideas (III.i–ii; cp. III.xi.11: 514). But this is not to say that experience cannot set up a connection between a word and the idea it is used to indicatively signify such that one passes from the sound of the word to that idea without making an inference. Indeed, this is precisely the kind of laziness that Locke thinks responsible for so much confusion. Consider the case of a person who has already mastered one language attempting to learn another. On Locke's view there is a two-step process. First, one tries to infer the ideas a speaker has in his mind. We can check our progress, Locke thinks, by means of ostensive definition. After a time, a different kind of connection is set up, this time, not between a word and the idea in the speaker's mind, but between the word and an idea in one's own mind, with which one customarily associates that idea. Locke writes,

there comes by constant use, to be such *a Connexion between certain Sounds, and the* Ideas *they stand for*, that the Names heard, almost as readily excite certain *Ideas*, as if the Objects themselves, which are apt to produce them, did actually affect the Senses . . . [B]y familiar use from our Cradles, we come to learn certain articulate Sounds very perfectly, and have them readily on our Tongues, and always at hand in our Memories . . . (III.ii.6,7: 407; see II.viii.7: 134)

So after constantly conjoining a word with an idea, our thoughts move without hesitation from the one to the other. Locke never says that this activity is signification. Indeed, the causal connection presupposes, and so cannot explain, the conventional link established through signification.

> Words, by their immediate Operation on us, cause no other *Ideas*, but of their natural Sounds: and 'tis by the Custom of using them for Signs, that they excite, and revive in our Minds latent *Ideas*; but yet only such *Ideas*, as were there before. For Words seen or heard, re-call to our Thoughts those *Ideas* only, which to us they have been wont to be Signs of: But cannot introduce any perfectly new, and formerly unknown simple *Ideas*. (IV.xviii.3: 689)

Even if a man were inspired by God, he could not communicate to others any simple ideas they have not already had. This, as we have seen, was precisely Augustine's point: words do not magically transmit any content; they serve only to indicate ideas in the mind of the speaker, or to revive ideas in us. What is crucial for our purposes is the clear relation of dependence Locke draws between words as causes of ideas in the hearer's mind and words as indicators. It is only in virtue of their role as signs of ideas in the speaker's minds that they are able to revive ideas in us. As we shall see below, the latter practice is a kind of laziness that, in some contexts, is pernicious.

Before we can move on to see how Locke argues for the thesis that words signify nothing but ideas, we must clear up two other issues. I have noted above that Locke is very free in his terminology: he sometimes says that words "denominate" or "name" things, and his talk of words primarily signifying ideas has led Kretzmann and Ashworth to supply him with a notion of secondary signification. Does Locke think that the indicative signification of ideas is the only, or even the central, role played by words?

Let us begin with primary and secondary signification. Both Kretzmann and Ashworth claim, reasonably enough, that the passages early on in Book III (esp. III.ii.1: 405; III.ii.2: 405; III.ii.4: 406; III.ii.8: 408) commit Locke to a distinction between these two kinds of signification. But in the course of Book III, Locke lets the restriction to primary or immediate signification drop, claiming simply that words are "the Signs of our *Ideas* only" (III.x.15: 499). Moreover, he never so much as uses the phrases "mediate" or "secondary" signification; still less does he explain these notions.

Traditionally, the distinction between primary and secondary signification was drawn in order to set apart ideas and things as distinct classes of significates of words. This distinction is easily accommodated on my account, for Hobbes specifies a sense (albeit a degenerate one) in which one may say that words signify things. Hobbes writes, "for that the sound of this word *stone* should be the sign of a stone, cannot be understood in any sense but this, that he that hears it collects that he that pronounces it thinks of a stone."[78] We must note, as Kretzmann and Ashworth do not, that Locke claims that words *"properly* and immediately signify" (III.ii.4: 406, my emphasis; see III.ii.7: 407) nothing but ideas, implying that they can only *im*properly be said to signify things. If my suggestion is correct, we can easily see why Locke would say this, for only in an attenuated sense can we say that words signify things.[79]

Even if we accept this, however, we must acknowledge that Locke often speaks, in other contexts, of words "denominating" things; we are said to "rank things under names" (see, e.g., III.iii.13: 415; III.vi.1: 438). Does Locke, then, have room for a semantic relation between words and extra-mental things, in addition to the semiotic relation between words and ideas? This question is difficult to answer precisely because Locke is so loose in his terminology. For he often says that words "name" ideas (II.xi.8–9: 158–9; III.vi.6: 442; III.vii.1: 471). Moreover, he tells us nothing about what this other semantic category is supposed to be. Certainly "naming" cannot be reference; otherwise, Locke would be guilty of holding semantic idealism. I think it is most reasonable, in light of Locke's linguistic thesis and the emphasis he puts on it, to read the "denomination" of things by words as reducible to the signification of ideas. There are three key considerations here. First, since Locke says nothing by way of arguing for or even explicating the claim that words denominate or name things, it is difficult to see how we could be justified in interpreting him as undertaking a commitment to an altogether new semantic category. Second, Locke can reduce the denomination of things to the signification of ideas in the way suggested above: to say that "x" denominates *x* is just to say that someone uttering "x" is indicating that she has *x* in mind. And if my reading is correct, it is hardly surprising that Locke should require a shorthand for this cumbersome analysis. Finally, as we shall see, Locke spends a great deal of time in III.x and elsewhere deploying the linguistic thesis against the Aristotelian. If he did think that words refer to extra-mental things, it is very hard to understand why he would do so, for he would no longer be disagreeing with the Aristotelian: both could happily claim that words refer to things. By contrast, Locke believes that striving for Aristotelian

---

[78] *De Corpore* I.ii.5 (1839–45, vol. 1, p. 17).

[79] It is also worth noting that Sergeant attributes to Locke the view that words signify ideas in the mind of the speaker; nowhere does Sergeant mention primary/immediate, or secondary/mediate signification. In his marginal notes, Locke very often corrects what he perceives as misconstruals of his position. But he is silent on this point.

real definitions is a result of misunderstanding the role of words as signs of ideas. (I do not suppose that this last consideration can be persuasive until chapter four, where we explore Locke's anti-Aristotelian argument in detail.)

At a minimum, then, it seems we can ascribe to Locke the position that for speech to have sense requires (a) a suitable convention and (b) an intention to communicate by participating in that convention (III.i.2: 402; III.ii.2: 405). What is necessary on the hearer's side? First let us ask what it is to understand other kinds of conventional sign. What is it to understand, for example, what a stone at the boundary of a field means? It is at least this: (c) to take it as a sign of the boundary of a field, and (d) to be *correct* in so taking it, (c) will be possible only if one has knowledge of the convention invoked in (a), whereas (d) depends on (b) the intentions of the person, if such there be, who put the stone there. Similarly, we might say that to understand speech is for the hearer (c) to take the words as indicative signs of ideas in the mind of the speaker (or mental acts), and (d) to be correct in so taking them. Although Locke doesn't use this terminology, it seems that when we simply allow words to revive ideas in us, we cannot really be said to be engaged in communication, even if doing so is sufficient for daily life.

This notion of signification as indication is radically different from that of sense or reference, or making known, or expressing. But this does not entail that the notion of signification found in these authors is not properly called "meaning." There is a perfectly good pre-theoretical sense of "meaning" that fits the bill: a motorist can ask a mechanic, "what does this green puddle mean?", without using "mean" in a novel sense. The view will seem alien to us only so long as we fail to keep in mind the logical and explanatory priority these writers thought the mental had over the linguistic. On Locke's view, the work of intentionality is carried out at the level of ideas. If we must speak in terms of sense and reference (and I do not see why), we must say that if anything, *ideas* have sense; that is, they are or have a "mode of presenting" an object, and reference, a thing or class of things falling under them. On this account, words do not magically latch on to things through some unspecified causal connection. They are of use only in unfolding our minds to one another.

LOCKE'S MAIN ARGUMENT

Hobbes's understanding of what it is for a word to be a sign provides him with a very straightforward argument for the conclusion that words cannot be signs of things:

But seeing names ordered in speech . . . are signs of our conceptions, it is manifest they are not signs of the things themselves; for that the sound of this word *stone* should be the sign of a stone, cannot be understood in any sense but this, that he that hears it collects that he that pronounces it thinks of a stone. And, therefore, that disputation, whether words signify matter or form, or something compounded of both, and other like subtleties of the *metaphysics*, is kept up by erring men, and such as understand not the words they dispute about.[80]

If we read "signify" as "express" or "refer" or any of the other candidates Ashworth brings forward as common currency among the late Scholastics, the dispute Hobbes refers to makes some sense. Its connection with the detested hylomorphist framework is clear enough: is the substance itself, a form/matter compound, referred to or expressed by our words, or do words pick out some one of these elements? Hobbes dismisses the controversy with one stroke: once we understand what signification really is, and so under- stand the words we dispute about, we can see that it would be absurd to claim that anything besides our own cogitations were the significates of words. The argument is simple: if "sign" is understood as Hobbes defines it, "stone" cannot signify a stone. For to do so it would have to be a harbinger, as it were, or an indication, of a stone. Unless I am a magician, stones do not ap- pear when I utter the word "stone." If I wanted my utterance "stone" to be a sign of stones, I would have to be very sparing in my use of the word.

Armed with this grasp of one important contemporary understanding of "signification," as well as with Hobbes's argument to the effect that words do not signify extra-mental objects, we are now in a position to come to grips with Locke's argument in favor of his linguistic thesis.

Kretzmann quotes an argument he takes to be another version of the argument from representative ideas, but which his account is powerless to explain. Locke writes, "by this tacit reference to the real Essence of that Species of Bodies, the Word *Gold* . . . comes to have no signification at all, being put for somewhat, whereof we have no *Idea* at all, and so can signify nothing at all, when the Body itself is away" (III.x.19: 501). I shall explore the context of this passage at greater length below (chapter four). For now, let us see whether either of the two dominant interpretations can make sense of its argument.

If we take the primary signification of a word as its sense, and its mediate or secondary signification as its reference, as Kretzmann's account seems to suggest, there is, perhaps, a good reason why one cannot give a word the latter without also giving it the former. How could anyone refer to

---

[80] *De Corpore* I.ii.5 (1839–45, vol. 1, p. 17).

something if there were no mode in which that thing was presented to him, or, to use Gareth Evans's terminology, how could one think about something without there being a *way* in which one thinks about that thing?[81] If we were to cash out Locke's view in this way, we might read him as saying that our words cannot succeed in referring to things when they lack sense.

But this sort of argument is not to be found in the passage at hand. Why should it be that, if one uses a word to signify something without the mediation of an idea, that word would signify nothing "when the Body itself" was away? What difference could *that* possibly make? If sense and reference have any place here, the conclusion should be that it is in principle *impossible* to primarily signify a thing (as opposed to an idea) with a word, not that, if one did so, the signification would only work when the thing signified was present. Alternatively, the Kretzmannian might say that "when the Body itself is away" is to be read as "when the thing one is attempting to refer to does not exist." Thus Locke would be warning us that successful reference can take place only when the referent exists; this view, if counterintuitive and perhaps false, is at least intelligible. But this is not Locke's point at all: for a body to be away seems to be nothing more than for the body to be out of the presence of the speaker.[82]

Nor does Ashworth's view fare any better here. To say that "signify" in this passage is used by Locke to include aspects of both sense and reference does not enable us to explain why it should be that this combination does not obtain when the thing signified is out of the presence of the speaker. We might read Ashworth as suggesting instead that "signify" is to be understood in the more general sense of "making something known." But why should the physical absence of a thing impede one's ability to make it known to others through words? The proposal under fire from Locke seems to be that words can (immediately) signify real essences of things. Why should someone putting forth that proposal be vulnerable to the objection that the word could only do its work of making known the real essence when the body whose real essence is at issue is present?[83] Moreover, on Ashworth's account, Locke is saying that one cannot signify a thing unless one has an

---

[81] See Gareth Evans (1982, p. 32ff.).   [82] See III.vi.19: 449.

[83] It has been suggested to me that Ashworth and/or Kretzmann might respond by saying that the presence of the body allows one to have an idea that determines the thing the name signifies ostensively. While this might explain why the body must *at some time or other* be "present" so that one can have an idea of it, it cannot, on pain of denying our ability to remember ideas, explain why the word cannot signify anything when the body is away. Another ingenious response worth considering is this: in the absence of an idea of a real essence of, say, gold, one purporting to signify that essence by his words can only have in mind ideas such as "yellow," "malleable," etc. Thus when the piece of gold is removed, the claim that one is speaking about its real essence seems plausible only because these ideas can be recalled – "gold" calls up this collection of ideas. But on this story,

idea of it. But in this passage, Locke implies that if the thing were present, one *could* signify it, even in the absence of an idea.

In fact, the only way to understand this passage is to read "signify" as I have suggested. The proposal under consideration is that my word is a sign, not of any mental content or event in me, but rather of the hidden internal constitution of a thing. According to Locke, one does not have perceptual access to real essences; nevertheless, one might be able to infer that there are such things. This means that we might know that each individual instance of gold has *some* real essence, though we do not know what it is. This seems to allow that we could make a word a reliable indicator of the presence of the real essence of a thing simply because we know that a thing (which is perceptually accessible) and its real essence (which is not) come as a package. But Locke argues that this maneuver fails. For as long as the thing and its real essence cannot live up to the requirement that a word be able to reliably indicate them, the point about perceptual access is moot. The crucial criterion here is that they be the right sorts of things to be reliably indicated by words. This is explicit in the conclusion of Locke's argument: the word assumed to signify a real essence "can signify nothing at all, when the Body itself is away." Whether the word is supposed to be a sign of the thing or of the perceptually inaccessible real essence of the thing, the word will do its work only when its utterer is in the presence of that entity. This is absurd without being contradictory just because of the contingent fact that one, regrettably, cannot reliably indicate the presence of gold (or its real essence) simply by saying, "gold." This is the sense in which "gold" understood as signifying the real essence of gold, has "no signification at all."[84]

Let us consider another argument Locke offers against the idea that our words signify the real essences of things:

[T]hey not having any *Idea* of that real Essence in Substances, and their Words signifying nothing but the *Ideas* they have, that which is done by this Attempt, is only to put the name or sound, in the place and stead of the thing having that real Essence, without knowing what that real Essence is; and this is that which Men do, when they speak of Species of Things, as supposing them made by Nature, and distinguished by real Essences. (III.vi.49: 470)

According to the previous argument, the attempt to use "gold" to signify the real essence of a thing fails due to a set of contingent facts about the sorts

---

the word *does* have signification: it signifies a collection of ideas, even in the absence of the physical stuff. By contrast, Locke's conclusion is that the word *signifies nothing at all* when the body is away.

[84] See III.ii.7: 408, discussed above.

of things our words can reliably indicate. There is an alternative, however, to saying that "gold," given this signification, has no signification at all, and that is to say that the word signifies the auditory impression occasioned by the utterance of the word itself. This puts the "name or sound" of the word in place of the thing signified, which I take to mean, in the *role* of the thing signified.[85] If my uttering "gold" cannot be a reliable indicator of the presence of gold, it can, trivially, be a reliable indicator of the sound "gold." The word used in this way is not strictly speaking meaningless, since it signifies an idea; the idea in question is simply that of the sound of the word itself. Obviously, this is no improvement in the position of Locke's imaginary antagonist.

I think that the first of these arguments constitutes, albeit in a rather sketchy form, the basic line of thought Locke had in mind as support for his claim that words can signify nothing but ideas. On my reading, the thesis is this: all categorematic words conventionally signify (here, serve as grounds of inference for) nothing but ideas in the mind of the speaker. This follows from two premises: first, from the nature of signification, and second, from a set of contingent facts about what sorts of things words can be used to indicate. Locke thinks that he can rule out proposals that things other than ideas (and mental acts) are signified simply by consulting the definition of signification, and then seeing if these candidates can be linked with words in such a way as to meet that definition. Note that the argument I am attributing to Locke does not have the form of a reduction to contradiction: there is no logical impossibility about a world in which whenever anyone utters the word "stone," a stone appears. It is just that that world is not *our* world.

If I am right about Locke's argument in support of the thesis, the argument from the uses of words must be enlisted to support the first of the two premises I listed above. One naturally wants to say to Locke that, of course, *if* words are signs in Hobbes's sense, then there will be a difficulty in making them signs of anything but ideas or acts of the mind; but why believe that words are signs in this sense? Locke's response will be to advert to the uses to which words are put: insofar as communication is what is wanted, he will argue that words must be signs of ideas.

We can now round out this discussion by re-examining the passage in which Kretzmann purports to find the "argument from representative ideas" (III.ii.2: 405). Immediately before the portion quoted above, Locke

---

[85] In this connection, compare Arnauld and Nicole (1970, p. 67): "Car il y auroit de la contradiction entre dire que je sais ce que je dis en pronançant un mot, & que neanmoins je ne conçois rien en le prononançant que le son même du mot."

states both the linguistic thesis and the argument from the uses of words. With this in place, he can then argue that it is impossible for someone to use words to (immediately) signify anything but ideas. Locke argues that "this would be to make them Signs of his own Conceptions, and yet apply them to other *Ideas*, which would be to make them Signs, and not Signs, of his *Ideas* at the same time." Before we can understand this argument we must be clear about what else such a speaker is trying to signify. The rest of the passage suggests that the "other *Ideas*" Locke intends are ideas in the minds of others. The violation of the thesis, then, lies in the attempt to make one's words signs of one's ideas and those of others at once. There is nothing contradictory in this; however, the nature of signification together with obvious facts about distinct human minds entails that such an attempt must fail. As Locke says at the end of the passage, even if the speaker "consents to give [his ideas] the same Names, that other Men do, 'tis still to his own *Ideas*; to *Ideas* that he has, and not to *Ideas* that he has not" (III.ii.2: 406). Moreover, the purpose of speech is to reveal one's mind to others, not to reveal *other* minds to others. This is what gives the violation of the thesis Locke considers its air of self-contradiction. If my interpretation is correct, there is no need to attribute the fallacious argument from representative ideas to Locke; instead, this passage draws out one consequence of the nature and purpose of linguistic signification, viz., that the sole proper objects of such signification are one's own ideas.

I believe that my interpretation is to be preferred simply because it better accords with the texts. Historians of philosophy who want to attribute to Locke views that, if not ultimately correct, are at least plausible by our lights, will initially look askance at my view: although I have argued against attributing to him the fallacious argument examined above, the interpretation I defend must sound harsh to the ears of philosophers steeped in the Fregean tradition. For at bottom there is no room for an irreducible conception of *Bedeutung* in Locke's view. He can recast sentences involving ascriptions of reference easily enough, but he cannot, and does not wish to, accommodate the intuition that words directly refer to things. This is the heart of his disagreement with the Aristotelians. Insofar as one's sympathies lie with a Kripke/Putnam view of reference, one is apt to find Locke's position absurd. But it is worth noting that Locke is no less out of step with causal theories of reference when it comes to the intimately related issue of natural kinds, an issue I shall turn to below in chapter three.

CHAPTER 2

Particles and propositions

Before we can proceed to apply Locke's views on language to other topics, we must fill a lacuna that has been left by the preceding chapter. So far we have seen nothing at all from Locke about the crucial issues of propositional content and attitude. If we were to take Locke at his word in the early chapters of Book III, his position would be hopelessly unable to account for the feature that differentiates a proposition from a mere list of items, and for whatever differentiates such propositional attitudes as belief, doubt, supposition, and so on. As we shall see, Locke's position has the resources to meet these demands.

Locke states his linguistic thesis in Book III as if it applied to all words whatsoever. But even if we grant that nouns and predicates signify ideas (confining ourselves to declarative sentences), it is hardly plausible to think that words such as "is," "and," and "but" work in this way.[1] There is a hoary tradition that runs from Aristotle (*De Interpretatione* 16b20 and 20a13) through the medievals and early moderns that distinguishes "categorematic" words (such as nouns and predicates), which can be significant on their own, from "syncategorematic" words, such as those listed above, which cannot.[2] Into the latter class fall the logical connectives, the copula, and prepositions, among others. The difficulty with Locke's view is that it seems to have no place for syncategoremata. The central case we shall examine is that of the copula. If Locke held that "is" signified an idea, his account would not only be phenomenologically implausible but unable to account for what Peter Hylton calls "the unity of the proposition." What is it that makes a set of words (and the ideas they signify) into a proposition rather than a list?

I shall argue that Locke implicitly restricts the thesis to categoremata. On his view, like that of his immediate predecessors the Port-Royalians, the copula signifies not an idea but a mental act that unites the ideas in

---

[1] See William P. Alston (1964, p. 24). This objection is very popular. See, e.g., Simon Blackburn (1984, p. 48) and Tim Crane (1995, ch. 1).
[2] This tradition is catalogued in Nuchelmans (1986).

a mental proposition. This, however, raises a new problem. For the Port-Royalians refer to this act of combination as "judgment." How, then, can they make sense of propositional attitudes other than assent? If in connecting the subject and the predicate one is thereby judging, how is it possible to withhold assent, or to suppose something for the sake of argument? A number of philosophers, including Mill, Peter Geach, and Anthony Kenny, have claimed the moderns' accounts of language are vitiated by their inability to account for the propositional attitudes. In this historiographical tradition, Frege (or perhaps Kant) is seen as the first philosopher to draw a serviceable distinction between proposition and attitude. By contrast, I shall locate Locke's views in a continuous chain of development that runs from the Port-Royal logicians to Kant and Frege. Locke can be blamed for his relative neglect of propositional attitudes, but his embryonic account has much more in common with those of Kant and Frege than has been recognized.

I am not claiming that Locke's view is fully defensible. Indeed, I shall argue that his account of affirmation and negation is subtly circular. Nevertheless, the difficulties to which it succumbs are quite other than those usually diagnosed.

THE COPULA AND PROPOSITIONAL CONTENT

We must begin by setting out more clearly the problem of propositional unity. This was felt acutely by the Russell of the early years of the century, as Hylton argues, as well as by Wittgenstein in the *Tractatus*.[3] Here is Russell's statement of the problem:

Consider, for example, the proposition "A differs from B." The constituents of this proposition, if we analyze it, appear to be only A, difference, B. Yet these constituents, thus placed side by side, do not reconstitute the proposition. The difference which occurs in the proposition actually relates A and B, whereas the difference after analysis is a notion which has no connection with A and B. It may be that we ought, in the analysis, to mention the relations which difference has to A and B, relations expressed by *is* and *from* when we say "A is different from B." These relations consist in the fact that A is referent and B relatum with respect to difference. But "A, referent, difference, relatum, B" is still merely a list of terms, not a proposition.[4]

If we attempt to construct a proposition out of simple elements (whether ideas or Russellian "terms"), we are bound to fail, for in addition to these

[3] See Wittgenstein (1974, Proposition 3.141ff.)
[4] Russell (1937b, §54); quoted in Hylton (1984, p. 376).

elements we require a means of uniting them in a proposition. This problem does not seem tied to any particular view of reference or meaning. Indeed, Locke's account of signification makes the problem more pressing: to say that all words signify ideas closes off any possibility of introducing propositional unity.

The problem becomes clearer if we examine an objection Peter Geach lodges against Hobbes. In his *De Corpore*, Hobbes claims that there is no necessity that a proposition be composed of subject, copula, and predicate. It is possible to get by without the copula with sufficient conventions that accomplish the same task by, say, the order of the words.[5] Remarking on this position, Peter Geach writes, "Hobbes . . . held that the copula was superfluous; but we might very well object that on the contrary it is necessary, because a pair of names is not a proposition but a list . . .".[6] This comment of Geach's is useful, even if it misses the point of Hobbes's declaration of the superfluity of the copula. For Hobbes's idea is simply that, while the job of the copula must be done, it need not be done by "is," "est," or what have you. His point here is surely sound. We could in principle accomplish the same task by writing the name of the subject above the name of the predicate on the page, or by clearing our throats before speaking the two words; we would be "not a jot the less capable of inferring, concluding, and of all kinds of reasoning, than were the Greeks, and Latins."[7] So far from making a proposition into a list by analyzing each of its members as categorematic terms, Hobbes explicitly states that the copula is not a name at all.[8] This becomes clear if we examine Hobbes's view of the proposition:

A Proposition *is a speech consisting of two names copulated, by which he that speaketh signifies he conceives the latter name to be the name of the same thing whereof the former is the name; or* (which is all one) *that the former name is comprehended by the latter*. (*De Corpore* I.iii.2)[9]

For Hobbes, the copula's function is to indicate that the speaker is conceiving of things in a certain manner. This accords well with the primacy of the mental over the linguistic: the function of the verbal proposition is to serve as a spoken sign of internal conceptions, and one important aspect of this is to signify the *way* in which the speaker is having those conceptions.

---

[5] *De Corpore* I.iii.2 in Hobbes (1839–45, vol. 1, p. 31).   [6] Geach (1980, p. 60).
[7] *Leviathan* IV.46 (1839–45, vol. 3, p. 674).   [8] *Ibid.*
[9] Hobbes (1839–45, vol. 1, p. 30). See also *Leviathan* IV.46 in Hobbes (1839–45, vol. 3, pp. 673–4) and *Human Nature* V.9 in Hobbes (1839–45, vol. 4, p. 23).

Nor, of course, do the Port-Royalians think of propositions as lists of ideas. As we have seen, they agree with Locke that words "are distinct and articulated sounds that people have made into signs to indicate what takes place in the mind."[10] On their view, the greatest distinction we can draw among what passes in the mind lies between objects of thought and the form or manner in which we think them.[11] Correspondingly, in addition to words that indicate that we are thinking of a given thing, we must have words that indicate the manner in which we think of it. In particular, a verb "is nothing other than *a word whose principal function is to signify an affirmation.*"[12] Affirmation is an act performed on two ideas and is the principal mode of our thought. It is, however, only the verb "to be," and that only in the third person, that works in this limited way: other verbs are also used to express ideas. The suggestion here is that verbs other than "to be," although they signify affirmation (since they can always be construed as involving the copula: e.g., "Peter lives" says the same thing as "Peter is living"), can also be used to express attributes (as "is living" expresses the attribute of living as well as affirmation). And although

not all our judgments are affirmative, since there are also negative judgments, verbs nonetheless always signify in themselves only affirmations, negations being indicated only by the particles "not" and "no," or by nouns including them, *nullus*, *nemo*, "none," "no one." When joined to verbs, these words change them from affirmations to negations . . .[13]

On this view, negation is signified by adding a negative particle or noun to a verb that by itself signifies affirmation. It is crucial that verbs indicate the *activity* of affirmation, and not the idea of it; it is an act, not another object of thought alongside the others. In Scholastic terms, we might say that affirmation and negation are operations of judgment, while the concepts or ideas *affirmation* and *negation* are "second intentions" that have as their objects these first-order operations.[14] The case of interjections provides a parallel. There is a great difference between "yahoo" and "joy," even though in a sense they signify the same feeling. A sincere utterer of the former expresses an emotion he is actually having, while an utterer of the latter is signaling that he is thinking of joy, and obviously need not be

---

[10] Arnauld and Nicole (1996, p. 74; see p. 37).   [11] Arnauld and Lancelot (1966, p. 47).
[12] Arnauld and Nicole (1996, p. 79). By contrast, Dickoff and James (Arnauld and Nicole, 1964, p. 104) translate this definition thus: "a verb is nothing else but a word whose principal function is to indicate assertion." But this is to conflate assertion and affirmation, and Dickoff and James are simply wrong to translate *affirmer* as assertion.
[13] Arnauld and Nicole (1996, p. 82).
[14] For another treatment of these issues, see Nuchelmans (1983, p. 76).

in the grip of that emotion.[15] The copula signifies the act of affirmation, which makes the difference between merely conceiving of a subject and a predicate on one hand and combining or separating them in a proposition on the other. The nature of affirmation "is to unite and identify, so to speak, the subject with the attribute, since this is what is signified by the word 'is'."[16]

Given the sense of signification common to Hobbes and the Port-Royalians, this makes a good deal of sense. Just as a categorematic word indicates the corresponding idea in the mind of the speaker, so the particle indicates the corresponding act. Locke's discussion of particles in III.vii comes into focus when seen against this background. In a mental proposition, the mind, "either by perceiving or supposing the Agreement or Disagreement of any of its *Ideas*, does tacitly within it self put them into a kind of Proposition affirmative or negative . . ." (IV.v.6: 576). Among other things, particles serve to indicate these acts of the mind.[17] These acts, which Locke has "endeavoured to express by the terms *Putting together* and *Separating*" (ibid.), are responsible for introducing propositional content and distinguishing between a mere concatenation of ideas, as when one thinks of a golden mountain, and a proposition, wherein ideas are related in a complex that admits of a truth-value. Locke echoes *La Grammaire* II.xiii (cp. *La Logique* II.ii)[18] when he writes,

Besides Words, which are names of *Ideas* in the Mind, there are a great many others that are made use of, to signify the *connexion* that the Mind gives to *Ideas, or Propositions, one with another*. The Mind, in communicating its thought to others, does not only need signs of the *Ideas* it has then before it, but others also, to shew or intimate some particular action of its own, at that time, relating to those *Ideas*. This it does in several ways; as, *Is*, and *Is not*, are the general marks of the Mind, affirming or denying. But besides affirmation, or negation, without which, there is in Words no Truth or Falsehood, the Mind does, in declaring its Sentiments to others, connect, not only the parts of Propositions, but whole Sentences one to another, with their several Relations and Dependencies, to make a coherent Discourse. (III.vii.1: 471)[19]

---

[15] For a discussion of the distinction between interjections and categoremata as it was found in the medieval literature, see Nuchelmans (1983, p. 55ff.)

[16] Arnauld and Nicole (1996, p. 129).

[17] Thus I disagree with Jonathan Bennett, who claims that Locke's treatment of particles "amounts to a depiction of them as classificatory after all" (1971, p. 20).

[18] "Les hommes . . . n'ont pas eu moins besoin d'inventer des mots qui marquassent l'affirmation . . . que d'inventer qui marquassent les objets de nos pensées" (1980, p. 175).

[19] It is worth noting that Russell sometimes offers a similar account of syncategoremata. For instance, he writes, "my statement ['that was a stoat or a weasel'] expresses partial knowledge combined with hesitation; the word 'or' expresses my hesitation, not something objective" (1948, p. 126).

Like Hobbes and the Port-Royalians, Locke insists that the copula does not function as categorematic words do. For instead of signifying an idea, it signifies an act of the mind, which is responsible for connecting ideas and forming a proposition. Through reflection, one gains an idea of affirmation; but this idea is not what is signified by the copula.

It is worth pausing to note that this provides further support for my interpretation of Lockean signification. It is not clear how other interpretations, such as that of Kretzmann, can come to grips with III.vii. Kretzmann is, in effect, faced with a dilemma: either particles are words lacking sense (since they are not correlated with any ideas), or there is another kind of signification at issue besides sense or reference. But matters are still worse, since even if one allows that a particle term can refer to an act of the mind without signifying an idea, the view this generates falls prey to the argument set out above: a proposition composed solely of referring terms does not seem to be a proposition at all. On my interpretation, there is no need to postulate a new sense of signification to accommodate what Locke says at III.vii.

It is true, however, that Locke's claim that particles signify mental acts conflicts with the linguistic thesis insofar as it admits that some words signify acts rather than ideas; as we shall see below (chapter six), this was one source of inspiration for Berkeley as he struggled against the thesis in its unrestricted form. But this tension within Locke's text is best seen as arising from the different purposes he has in these passages. At the start of Book III, he is beginning to sketch his own view of essences and laying the groundwork for his attack on the Aristotelians in III.x. There he is simply not concerned with the detailed workings of language. The focus is on sortal terms, not on propositions or their syncategorematic components. In III.vii he makes clear that his view can make sense of non-categorematic terms and can account for the unity of the proposition.

It is worth noting that Locke's treatment of the copula departs from that of the Port-Royalians. On their view, "is" always signifies affirmation; by adding "not" one as it were deflects this affirmation into a negation. Locke, by contrast, treats "is not" as a single element, signifying negation. This seems much more plausible; Locke does not posit an act of affirmation contained within the act of negation. Locke's account is also richer than is usually recognized. For under the heading of particles he includes other syncategorematic elements that indicate mental acts other than combination and separation. Locke claims that in addition to the copula, senseful discourse requires a battery of other words to indicate "the several Postures of [the] Mind in discoursing" (III.vii.3: 472). In addition to the more familiar logical connectives, Locke offers a subtle analysis of "but," discussing five distinct uses of it to "intimate several relations, the Mind gives to the several Propositions or Parts of them, which it joins by this monosyllable" (III.vii.5: 473). For example, in the proposition "you pray, but it is not that God would bring you to the true religion," "but" "intimates a supposition in the Mind, of something otherwise than it should be" (ibid.) In this use, the word conveys censure. This is not another idea alongside the constituents of the proposition, nor does it contribute to the truth-value of the sentence, since here "but" simply has the force of a conjunction. Nevertheless, the word allows the speaker to convey the manner or way in which he conceives of the proposition.

I have up till now been defending Locke's view from an obvious objection. It will now emerge that although Locke is justified in holding that particles signify acts of the mind, the account he offers of these acts is in fact circular. We have been taking for granted such notions as "combining" and "separating" one's ideas. These activities allow mental propositions to admit of truth values. In this, Locke is following a tradition stemming from Aristotle, who says that "names and verbs by themselves – for instance "man" and "white" when nothing further is added – are like the thoughts that are without combination and separation; for so far they are neither true nor false" (*De Interpretatione* 16a14–15).[20] But obviously mere reliance on a tradition does not absolve a philosopher of the duty to give a satisfactory working-out of his position. If Locke cannot give an account of these notions that does not presuppose the presence of propositional content, his view is uninformative. This, I shall argue, is precisely the situation in which we find him.

What does Locke mean by his metaphor of combination? Let us first make sure we know what it *cannot* mean. Combination cannot merely be a matter of holding two ideas in the mind at once, for this is equally true of the separation involved in negation. Moreover, if combination were understood in this way, then other operations on simple ideas[21] (such as those by which we construct our idea of God, for example) would have to involve affirmation. Nor can combination mean simply conflating one's ideas; for then one has a mongrel idea, not a proposition.

Locke thinks that whether combination or separation takes place depends on whether one takes the ideas to agree (combination) or disagree (separation). To "combine" ("separate") one's ideas in this sense, it seems,

---

[20] In Aristotle (1984, vol. 1, p. 25).
[21] See, e.g., II.xii.2: 164 for a discussion of these other operations.

is to judge that two ideas do (do not) agree. At IV.i.2: 524, Locke sets out four kinds of agreement or disagreement that might obtain between ideas: identity or diversity, relation, co-existence, and real existence. We have a fourfold concatenation of kinds of proposition and truth-value: (a) an affirmative judgment that is true in virtue of one of these kinds of agreement; (b) an affirmative judgment that is false because this agreement does not obtain; (c) a negative judgment that is true because its ideas do not agree, and (d) a negative judgment that is false because its ideas do in fact agree. This kind of agreement or disagreement is supposed to be available in introspection, and we know it via intuition (IV.iii.8: 543–4).[22] Sometimes, of course, we need to introduce intervening ideas in order to perceive such agreement or disagreement (IV.ii.2–3: 531–2).

But how enlightening is this as an analysis of negation? To perform a negation is to separate one's ideas, i.e., to judge that the two ideas do not agree, where this in turn is analyzed in one of the four ways above. But these analyses themselves invoke negation; they themselves have propositional content. To take one example, consider the judgment φ: *that idea x does not contain idea y.* To judge that one's ideas disagree in this way is to make a judgment that already contains propositional content. Nor are matters helped by the appeal to intuition:[23] even if this is the means by which we ascertain the truth of a judgment such as φ, the fact remains that φ itself has propositional content and contains a negation. The same goes, *mutatis mutandis,* for the other varieties of combination and separation. Locke's account seems simply circular. Nor does there seem much hope for an alternative interpretation: the other ways we have looked at above that attempt to analyze "combination" and "separation" so as not to beg the question fail to introduce propositional content. Locke's only means of cashing out the metaphor of sub-propositional combination and separation presupposes what it is supposed to explain: propositional content.

PROPOSITIONAL ATTITUDES

Let us turn now to the second difficulty sketched above, that of propositional attitudes. At least since the time of J.S. Mill, it has often been said

---

[22] Thus Leibniz argues that Locke has not adequately specified the sort of agreement in question: "[a]greement obtains between two eggs, disagreement between two enemies" (*Nouveaux essais* IV.v.2, in Leibniz 1996, p. 311). Berkeley in his *Manuscript Introduction* to the *Principles* also criticizes Locke for not having specified what agreement is supposed to mean here.

[23] See II.xxi.5: 236, where Locke distinguishes three sorts of perception (the latter two of which he equates with understanding) according to their objects: of ideas, of the signification of signs, and of the agreement or disagreement of ideas.

that philosophers of the modern period are unable to account for propositional attitudes other than assent. For at first glance their views seem to provide little room for a distinction between the content of a proposition and the attitude one adopts toward it, be it doubt, disbelief, supposition for the sake of argument, or what have you.

Mill offers a sweeping condemnation of "[p]hilosophers, from the time of Descartes downwards, and especially from the era of Leibnitz and Locke," and indeed "almost all writers on Logic in the last two centuries, whether English, German, or French." They have made

> their theory of Propositions, from one end to the other, a theory of Judgments. They considered a Proposition, or a Judgment, for they used the two words indiscriminately, to consist in affirming or denying one *idea* of another. To judge, was to put two ideas together, or to bring one idea under another, or to perceive the agreement or disagreement between two ideas: and the whole doctrine of Propositions, together with the theory of Reasoning (always necessarily founded upon the theory of Propositions), was stated as if Ideas, or Conceptions, or whatever other term the writer preferred as a name for mental representations generally, constituted essentially the subject matter and substance of those operations . . . It is, of course, true, that in any case of judgment, as for instance when we judge that gold is yellow, a process takes place in our minds of which some one or other of these theories is a partially correct account. We must have the idea of gold and the idea of yellow, and these two ideas must be brought together in our mind. But in the first place, it is evident that this is only part of what takes place; for we may put two ideas together without any act of belief; as when we merely imagine something, such as a golden mountain; or when we actually disbelieve: for in order even to disbelieve that Mahomet was an apostle of God, we must put the idea of Mahomet and that of an apostle of God together.[24]

On Mill's view, the ideational treatment of language common to his predecessors led them to account for propositions in terms of the connection of ideas in an act of judging. Against this, Mill makes two points. First, since we often connect our ideas without thereby making a judgment at all, as when we merely imagine a golden mountain, it cannot be the case that all connection of ideas involves a proposition.[25] Second, Mill argues that if all propositions are judgments, we are left without any way to account for the diverse attitudes one might take up with respect to those propositions, such as doubting, hoping, supposing, etc. To equate propositions with judgments is to turn all propositional thought into belief. Thus

---

[24] Mill (1867, p. 59).

[25] Cp. Leibniz, who criticizes Locke by saying that "*l'homme sage*' does not express a proposition and is yet a joining of two terms, or, if one prefers, of the two ideas signified by those terms" (*Nouveaux essais* IV.v.2, in Leibniz 1996, p. 311).

the treatment of propositions common to the post-Cartesians is radically impoverished.

However acute his criticisms, it is not clear that Mill himself succeeds in distinguishing between propositional content and attitude, since he treats propositions and assertions as equivalent.[26] This erases the very distinction he chides the moderns for having failed to recognize.

Frege is the obvious choice to play the hero in this story. For Frege's distinction in *Begriffsschrift* between the content-stroke and the assertion-stroke does seem to sever, once and for all, propositional content from propositional attitude. In their respective works on Frege, Peter Geach and Anthony Kenny both present him as overthrowing the "traditional view," whereby all propositions are assertions. (I shall refer to this view without inverted commas even though I doubt whether it is traditional in any meaningful sense.) On the traditional view, Geach claims, a proposition is a subject/predicate complex, united by the copula; the view conflates this unification with assertoric force, with the result that all propositions make assertions. That the traditional view is wildly mistaken is almost too obvious to need pointing out: for example, some propositions serve as antecedents or consequents and so are not themselves asserted.[27] In this vein, Kenny writes that "some earlier logicians" had thought that "attaching a predicate to a subject . . . necessarily involve[s] making an assertion about what the subject named."[28] Neither Geach nor Kenny names any particular figure who is supposed to have held this view.

In a paper on the Port-Royal *Logic*, Jill Vance Buroker provides the best statement of the view I take to be natural to someone persuaded by this narrative. Buroker writes,

According to [the Port-Royalians], every time one connects a subject and a predicate, one is *ipso facto* judging. Thus there is no room for thinking propositions and suspending judgment, as Descartes advocated in his method of doubt. In fact the Port-Royal view of the copula would make this process impossible; for this reason Arnauld and Nicole use the terms "judgment" and "proposition" interchangeably . . . [Kant] takes the first step toward distinguishing judgment from proposition by treating the categories of modality – possibility, actuality, and necessity – as ways in which the proposition is held by the thinker. On Kant's view,

[26] See Mill (1867, p. 12) and Skorupski (1989, ch. 2).
[27] Geach writes, "[a] predicate may obviously be attached to a subject in a clause that does not serve to make an assertion" (1961, p. 133).
[28] Kenny (1994, p. 37). There is a potential confusion here between assertion, which seems to be a performance, and assent, which involves the ascription of an attitude. (To see the difference, recall that one may assert a proposition without assenting to it.) Nothing much turns on the issue, for my purposes.

problematic propositions express only logical possibility (A75/B101). Frege carries out the solution in the *Begriffsschrift* by distinguishing the content-stroke from the assertion-stroke, thereby removing assertive force entirely from the propositional content of the judgment.[29]

Call this the "progressivist" account: discussions of proposition and judgment in the modern period are benighted because of their inability to distinguish propositional content from attitude; Kant comes closer to the truth, but a robust distinction had to wait until Frege's *Begriffsschrift*.

I wish to undermine the progressivist account. I am not contesting the obvious fact that Frege represents a tremendous gain in clarity on these issues. What I *do* contest is the claim that, with the possible exception of Kant, Frege's modern predecessors were committed to the traditional view. Let me be clear about what my arguments must show. The progressivist need not, of course, claim that any figure explicitly made the error in question; more often, the suggestion seems to be that the error is entailed by other of the philosopher's commitments. Now, since the conflation of predication with assent or assertion is so obviously a confusion, it seems to me enough to show that a particular figure *need not* be read as making this conflation. If the argument for attributing this view to the figure in question is a poor one, only a minimal degree of charity is required to allow us to refrain from making the attribution. In the case of Locke, I argue that his text presents an embryonic account of propositional attitudes that not merely allows but compels us to refrain from foisting the traditional view on him.

Before beginning, a word of caution is in order about "judgment." The ambiguity of this word has caused much confusion. For my purposes, the most important distinction lies between the propositional and the subpropositional senses. In the former use, judgment involves an attitude toward a proposition. Thus for Descartes judgment always takes a proposition as its object: one judges *that* something is or is not the case.[30] This point is sometimes obscured by Descartes's use of "idea" to refer both to representations and propositions, although he says that only in the former sense is the term really appropriate.[31] On Descartes's view, intellectual perception provides us with an awareness of the proposition to be considered, while "various modes of willing," such as "desire, aversion, assertion, and denial" must be brought in to account for the attitude we adopt regarding the proposition.[32] Frege's use of "judgment" (*Urtheil*) clearly belongs

[29] Buroker (1993, p. 462).   [30] See, e.g., Descartes (1984, vol. 1, p. 45, p. 207; vol. 2, p. 26, p. 105).
[31] Descartes (1984, vol. 2, p. 25).   [32] Descartes (1984, vol. 1, p. 204).

in the propositional category as well. In his *Begriffsschrift*, a judgment is signified by a vertical stroke to the left of the content stroke. Removing the vertical stroke not only indicates that the content is not asserted, but also that the content is no longer a judgment but "*a mere complex of ideas*."[33] A content preceded by a horizontal stroke alone "will not express this judgment [that opposite magnetic poles attract one another], but should merely arouse in the reader the idea of the mutual attraction of magnetic poles, in order, say, to draw conclusions from it . . ."[34] Obviously, such "ideas" can be propositions, and can figure in deductions, or, as Frege sometimes says, "pseudo-deductions."[35] Despite their differences, both the Cartesian and Fregean uses of judgment are propositional in that they assume that judgments take propositions as their objects.

We also find what I shall call the "sub-propositional" use of "judgment" in the modern period. It is in this sense that the Port-Royalians use it, or so I shall argue. Buroker is quite right to say that on their view, every time one entertains a proposition one is making a judgment. If they meant "judgment" in the propositional sense, they would obviously be open to refutation along Mill's lines. But if the progressivist takes for granted that propositional judgment is meant, she begs the question. This is something to be argued for, not assumed from the outset. In fact, on the Port-Royalian account, judgment is not something one does to a proposition, but rather to the *constituents* of propositions. On this view, judgment is a mental act in which one unites two ideas.

In discussing each text, then, it will be important to be clear about just what "judgment" means. Unless otherwise stated, I use "judgment" to mean the sub-propositional activity of uniting one's ideas. I shall now argue that this is the sense intended by the Port-Royalians.

We have already seen that "*affirmer*" refers to a mental act whereby we combine our ideas and so produce a judgment or proposition.[36] To say that I affirm *x* of *y* is simply to say that I am thinking of *x* and *y* in a particular manner: this is what it is to make a judgment. Affirmation, negation, and

---

[33] Frege (1997, p. 52).　　[34] Frege (1997, p. 53).

[35] Mitchell Green has pointed out to me that Fregean assertion/judgment requires not only that one genuinely hold that the asserted proposition is true, but that it actually be true. Frege often describes judgment as the recognition (*Anerkennen*) of a thought's truth. See, e.g., Frege (1980, pp. 20–2). *Anerkennen* is a success term: one cannot recognize that which is false. It seems, then, that to assert a false thought is only to seem to assert it, and to infer from a false thought is merely to make a "pseudo-inference" or a "purely formal deduction" (see Frege, 1980, p. 17). If this is correct, Buroker's reading of the purpose of Frege's assertion sign is mistaken. For it does not mark what we ordinarily call asserted propositions off from unasserted ones, simply because Frege also requires the content of an assertion to be a true thought. This is a difficult issue I do not pretend to settle here.

[36] Arnauld and Nicole (1996, p. 82).

their genus, judgment, are clearly sub-propositional acts and not acts that one performs upon a complete proposition.

We are not entitled to infer that all judgments are asserted. For assertion, unlike judgment in the Port-Royalian sense, must have a proposition as its object: one asserts propositions. But one does not *judge* propositions, in the sense Arnauld *et al.* specify. Their account so far says nothing at all about the assertive force of the resulting proposition. It is instead a view about how propositions are generated in the first place.

This is a key point in my argument. Let us pause to consider how Buroker goes wrong in reading the Port-Royalians as imbuing the copula with assertoric force. She attributes this mistake to them on the grounds of the following passage: "After conceiving things by our ideas, we compare these ideas and, finding that some belong together and others do not, we unite or separate them. This is called *affirming* or *denying*, and in general *judging*."[37] From this she deduces that "the copula has two functions in a judgment: it relates the subject and the predicate, and it signifies *affirmation* or *denial*."[38] But in order for this to support her interpretation, Buroker must read "affirming" and "denying" as carrying assertoric force. Have the Port-Royalians committed themselves to this? On the contrary, in the quoted text, they are using "affirming" and "denying" to refer to the sub-propositional act, and not the propositional attitude or the assertion of a proposition.

The progressivist might reply that even though affirmation and denial are sub-propositional, they still commit one to the resulting proposition. For in the text just quoted, Arnauld and Nicole claim that we compare our ideas and unite them in a proposition when we *find that* they agree or disagree. Does this not suggest that whenever we form a proposition, we also assent to it? We must keep in mind, however, that at this stage of their *Logic* (II, 3), the authors have not dealt with complex propositions. Among the latter are conditionals and counterfactuals. On the Port-Royalian view, in evaluating the truth of a proposition such as "if a creature's will can obstruct the absolute will of God, God is not omnipotent," "we consider only the truth of the inference."[39] In constructing the antecedent, we must unite our ideas; but we certainly cannot *find* that they agree, since, or so the Port-Royalians would presumably maintain, it is false that a creature's will can obstruct the will of God. But we nevertheless affirm this as part of an inference. Why should we think that Arnauld *et al.* hold, absurdly,

---

[37] Arnauld and Nicole (1996, p. 82).   [38] Buroker (1993, p. 460).
[39] Arnauld and Nicole (1996, p. 100).

that the affirmation contained in the antecedent has assertive force? To be sure, in order to entertain the antecedent, I must perform the mental act of combining these ideas. But this is to say nothing about the status of the proposition so formed.

Just as we cannot assume that every judgment containing an affirmation is asserted, so we cannot, *pace* Buroker, assume that every judgment containing a negation is a denial.[40] This, of course, would be disastrous: it would, for example, make it impossible to grasp a counterfactual, which has a false proposition as its antecedent. But again, there is no way to infer simply from a position about sub-propositional entities and acts to a position about propositional attitudes.

This is not to say that the Port-Royalians offer an adequate account of propositional attitudes. What I have done, at most, is to undermine the quick inference from sub-propositional act to propositional attitude. It remains to be seen whether the Port-Royalians have a satisfactory positive account.[41]

Rather than pursue this issue, let us return to Locke's account and see how it fares in the face of Mill's objections. Mill's first objection was that to connect our ideas is not thereby to make a judgment, since we might think of two ideas without making any judgment at all. This point is easily handled by Locke, Hobbes, and the Port-Royalians. For none claims that any act of connecting one's ideas whatsoever constitutes a judgment. It should be clear that, for Locke, not all separation of ideas is negation, for example, since at least one kind of abstraction is a process by which ideas are separated, and yet no proposition, mental or otherwise, is involved.[42]

What of Mill's second objection, viz., that in analyzing the connection the mind gives to its ideas in terms of negation and affirmation, this account makes all propositional thought assertoric? Part of the response to this

---

[40] Buroker (1993, p. 461).

[41] Arnauld *et al.* attempt to deal with at least some of the other attitudes one might take toward a proposition by means of inflection and mood: "I have said that the *principal* use of the verb is to signify affirmation, because we will see below that it is also used to signify other movements of our soul, such as *to desire, to pray, to command*, etc. But this is only to change the inflexion and the mood: and therefore we will consider the verb in this chapter only in its principal signification, which is the one which it has in the indicative . . ." (Arnauld and Lancelot, 1966, p. 109). Whatever these other movements of the soul might be, the verb's principal use is still to signify affirmation. In a later chapter in the *Grammaire* on the "moods or manners of verbs," the authors (1966, p. 121) argue that "beyond simple affirmations" such as "he loves," "there [are] some conditioned and some modified affirmations, such as *although he would have loved, when he would love*." To accommodate these acts of the mind, people doubled the inflections of some verbs in some tenses. But the authors do not provide any discussion of how this relates to the copula, beyond saying that they are "modified" affirmations.

[42] This is the model of abstraction to be found at, e.g., II.xi.9: 159. See below, chapter three.

objection has already been given. For Locke, like the Port-Royalians, sees affirmation and negation as sub-propositional. But a stronger defense can be made if we consider non-copulative particles such as "if" and "and." These signify relations between propositions and allow us to link propositions in chains of dependence and support. Such particles, then, can take as their objects propositions, which of necessity involve acts of combination and separation.

Already we have the materials to deal with negation as it occurs in counterfactuals. For on Locke's account, one constructs the antecedent, which is itself a proposition, by linking two signs of ideas with "is not," the sign of negation. When this proposition occurs after an "if" and is followed by another proposition, we have a third proposition which has as one of its constituents a proposition containing a negation. "If" signifies the connection one takes to obtain between the antecedent and the consequent. This alone should prevent us from thinking that Lockean negation is always denial, where this is understood as an attitude toward or operation on a proposition.[43]

The logical connectives do not exhaust the different ways in which the mind might consider propositions. Locke says that we give propositions "such different Entertainment, as we call *Belief, Conjecture, Guess, Doubt, Wavering, Distrust, Disbelief,* etc." (IV.xvi.9: 663). But what are these "entertainments?"

Locke seems to give two different answers. At the start of Book II, he declares them to be acts of the mind. His examples of the operations of the mind of which we have ideas of reflection are almost entirely made up of such attitudes: "*Perception, Thinking, Doubting, Believing, Reasoning, Knowing, Willing*" (II.i.4: 105). On this view, propositional attitudes are second-order acts having as their object propositions which themselves involve first-order acts (i.e., affirmation and negation).

But later in Book II, Locke lists "Believing, Doubting, Intending, Fearing, [and] Hoping" under the heading of "the several modes of Thinking" (II.xxiii.30: 313; see II.xix.1–4: 226–9). In calling propositional attitudes modes of thinking, Locke is making two points: that they are parasitic on the act of thinking a given proposition, which involves holding two ideas in mind and combining or separating them; and that they are ways in which one thinks of those propositions. If this is Locke's view, there is no need for a second-order act of the mind whose object is a proposition.

---

[43] Note that Locke himself in the passage quoted does not use "denial" in this technical sense. On his view, one can say both that an idea is denied of another idea, and that a proposition is denied. In the text I am using "denial" only in the latter sense.

Instead, if one is to think a proposition, there must be a *way* in which one thinks it; these different ways just are the propositional attitudes.

However that may be, it should be clear that Locke has not inadvertently made all propositions objects of affirmation or negation, nor has he confounded assertive force and propositional content. Propositions must *contain* such acts of the mind if they are to be propositions at all; but, *contra* the progressivist, assent does not exhaust the attitudes one might take up with regard to those propositions. The progressivist's objections stem from conflating affirmation with assertion or assent in a way Locke would find puzzling.

But as with the Port-Royalians, a problem arises in this context. Locke speaks of "perceiving, or judging" (IV.v.5: 575) that two ideas agree or disagree. This use of "judgment" is distinct from the official meaning Locke gives it, where it refers to the act of taking two ideas to agree or disagree when this is mediated by one or more other ideas, "whose certain Agreement, or Disagreement with them [the mind] does not perceive, but hath observed to be frequent or usual" (IV.xviii.17: 685). In the former use, it seems to commit one to the resulting proposition. After all, if one *perceives* the agreement of two ideas and so combines them in a proposition, how can one withhold assent? For Locke there are of course "intuitive" propositions such that the mind immediately perceives the agreement or disagreement of the constitutive ideas, "as the Eye doth light" (IV.ii.1: 531). Here it is impossible to withhold assent. The problem then is that in speaking of the perception of agreement or disagreement in IV.v.5, Locke is in danger of making all propositions intuitive. A little later in IV.v, Locke is more careful: he says that "whenever he [the thinker] *perceives, believes, or supposes*" (IV.v.6: 576; my italics) that his ideas agree or disagree, he combines or separates those ideas and so produces a proposition. This allows for combining or separating our ideas even when we doubt the resulting proposition, or know it to be false.

KANT AND THE MODALITY OF JUDGMENTS

Part of the progressivist's claim, although not an essential one, is that Kant represents a vast improvement over the moderns and a significant step on the road to Frege. Let us turn now, however briefly, to Kant's account, and test how far this progressivist story holds true.

Kant's table of judgments in the Analytic of Concepts includes four sets of three moments each under the headings of quantity, quality, relation, and modality. Under the last of these headings, Kant makes a set of distinctions that shows his sensitivity to the difference between propositional content and attitude.

It is crucial to see that what determines the modality of a judgment is the attitude of the judger: it is a matter of how one thinks of a given proposition.[44] To say that a judgment is possible is to report on the attitude of the judger, not to make a claim about *de re* modality. "Problematic judgments are those in which affirmation or negation is taken as merely possible (optional). In assertoric judgments affirmation or negation is viewed as real (true), and in apodeictic judgments as necessary" (A74/B100).[45] What counts, then, is the status one assigns to the judgment, which itself contains an affirmation or a negation. Kant claims that the modality of judgments "is a quite peculiar function" in that "it contributes nothing to the content of the judgment . . . but concerns only the value of the copula in relation to thought in general" (B99–100/A74).[46] Whether a judgment is problematic, assertoric, or apodeictic, it has precisely the same content. What one takes to be its relation to the laws of thought determines whether one considers a judgment as necessarily true, i.e., as following from the laws of thought, as simply true, or as possible.[47]

On Kant's view, the possibility of problematic judgments explains our ability to use false judgments as constituents of hypothetical judgments. In a proposition such as "if there is a perfect justice, the obstinately wicked are punished," the antecedent "is not stated assertorically, but is thought only as an optional judgment, which it is possible to assume; it is only the logical consequence which is assertoric. Such judgments may therefore be

---

[44] T.K. Swing writes, "[t]he problematic judgment is one whose truth is unknown or undetermined; the assertoric judgment is one whose truth is known or verified; and the apodeictic judgment is one whose truth is guaranteed by the laws of thought alone" (1969, pp. 17–18); quoted in Mattey (1986, p. 425, n. 10). Even this needs some correction, however, for Swing's characterization of apodeictic judgments omits the crucial feature that they are *taken* to be necessary truths. It is how judgments are viewed, not whether or not they in fact follow from any laws, that is at issue. Buroker also misses this point when she maintains for Kant problematic propositions "express only logical possibility" (1993, p. 462).

[45] Kant (1958, pp. 109–10).   [46] Kant (1958, p. 109).

[47] Here there arises a difficulty. For in what sense is a problematic judgment "merely possible?" There are two ways of taking this: first, as seems intended in the *Critique*, that an affirmation or negation is performed, but the act is regarded as optional, or alternatively, that no act of affirmation or negation is performed at all. The second view of problematic judgments seems to be adopted by Kant in the *Logic*, where he identifies assertoric judgments with propositions. (This, of course, is the very mistake Buroker lauds him for avoiding.) Kant (1974, p. 116) declares a "problematic proposition" to be a "*contradictio in adjecto.*" This is because "[b]efore I have a proposition I must indeed first judge" (*ibid.*) The difficulty is that if a problematic judgment is one in which no affirmation or negation is performed at all, then there will be no way to introduce propositional content. But in the *Critique*, the point is that the judger sees the act of affirmation or negation *which he has already performed* as optional, i.e., as not compelled by the laws of thought. For further discussion, see Mattey (1986, pp. 430–1).

obviously false, and yet, taken problematically, may be conditions of the knowledge of truth" (A75/B100).[48]

There is a non-trivial point of agreement here between Kant and Locke. For on Kant's account, the modality of a judgment reflects the attitude one adopts toward a sub-propositional act of affirmation or negation; similarly, Locke holds that the objects of propositional attitudes are mental propositions that of necessity contain acts of affirmation or negation. This is true whether Locke thinks that propositional attitudes are second-order acts or simply ways in which first-order acts (combination and separation) are performed.

Despite this, there is a significant difference between Kant and his predecessors. One difficulty with the mental act or mode account proposed by the early moderns is that it places no constraints whatever on what can be judged; to use Hylton's example, nothing rules out judging "that this table penholders the book."[49] Kant, by contrast, claims that the synthesis responsible for the unity of a judgment must be performed according to the categories.[50] Indeed, the categories just are the logical functions of judgment brought to bear on the manifold of representations (B143).[51] Since experience for Kant is shot through with judgment, as it were, this claim has an idealist consequence: our experiences could not be structured other than they are, simply because the categories constrain us in judgment, and experience is generated not by the impression of objects upon a passive understanding but by the understanding's actively structuring appearance in accordance with the categories, i.e., performing its characteristic function, judgment. It was in large measure Russell's wish to avoid the idealism implicit in so constraining judgment that led him to construct his own theories and to declare that "all sound philosophy should begin with an analysis of propositions."[52]

Obviously Kant's account raises many issues I have not space to explore here. For our purposes, the crucial point is that the same features of his view that prevent Kant from being landed with the traditional account are also to be found in his modern predecessors.

Although I of course do not pretend to have made a full survey of these issues in modern philosophy, I hope to have shown that the progressivist view is false. It is unfair to accuse the Port-Royalians of conflating affirmation (negation) with assertion or assent (denial). Locke's account provides a clear basis for marking off content from attitude, a basis on which Kant,

---

[48] Kant (1958, p. 110).   [49] Hylton (1984, pp. 386–7).
[50] Hylton (1984, pp. 378–92) argues for this claim in greater depth.   [51] Kant (1958, p. 160).
[52] Russell (1937a, p. 8), quoted in Hylton (1984, p. 375).

whether knowingly or not, builds. I do not claim that the moderns' account of the proposition is fully defensible. My claim is only that these figures cannot be convicted of subscribing to the traditional view. If I am right, the cleavage between the modern view and the proto-Fregean account of Kant is not so great as it at first seems. And this is precisely what one should expect.

CONCLUSION

In this chapter, I have been arguing that Locke's position does not succumb to the objections from propositional unity or attitude. In the latter case, there is a historiographical lesson to be learned. Narratives of the history of philosophy that turn on attributing fundamental mistakes to philosophers of an entire period are to be looked upon with suspicion. Locke's position is indeed subject to serious difficulties, but these problems do not flow from his having unthinkingly accepted an obviously false "traditional" view of propositional attitudes. Instead, they stem from his inability to provide an informative account of the mental acts that he thinks underlie verbal affirmation and negation.

CHAPTER 3

Essence and abstraction

Thus far, we have seen that for Locke, categorematic words signify ideas. The simple ideas given in sensation and reflection are all perfectly determinate, not only because their content is so, but also because each simple idea includes a "determination" to the particular time and place at which it was experienced (III.iii.6: 411). At first sight, this seems odd, as if each idea bore a sort of time-stamp linking it to the occasion on which it was given in sensation. Instead, Locke's point is that each simple idea is intromitted by the senses along with a number of other ideas, all of which together will determine that idea to a particular experiential context. If we had access only to such ideas, we would be correspondingly limited to thinking only about particulars. This is precisely the predicament of non-human animals, which, Locke suggests, are fully capable of reasoning. *Pace* Descartes, they are not mere automata; they can reason, but their reasoning is limited to particulars (II.xi.11: 160).

What is more, since each person's sensory and reflective ideas are determinate in both of the senses we have specified, limitation to particulars would make us unable to communicate. It would be impossible for different persons, each having distinct experiential histories, to use a word to signify the same idea (III.iii.3: 409–10).[1]

To remedy this predicament, Locke posits abstract ideas. But it is important to see that his discussion of abstraction is also an episode in his general anti-Aristotelian project. Abstraction functions as a replacement for the Aristotelian mechanism of intentionality, which was tied to the outmoded hylomorphist ontology. This raises the question of Locke's own ontological commitments with regard to properties and universals. Thus the second part of the present chapter is devoted to exploring the ontology underlying

---

[1] The earliest example of this criticism I have been able to find is in Henry Lee (1702, p. 43). Kant (1958, p. 182), makes a closely related objection to treating concepts as images. For the relevant sense of "same idea," see chapters one and six.

Locke's account of generality and essence. I shall argue that, far from being purely nominalist, Locke's thoroughgoing opposition to natural kinds is perfectly compatible with a kind of realism about properties. Although Locke attacks the idea of mind-independent essences, he happily endorses objective resemblances. Locke thus separates the issues of objective resemblance (and the properties that explain it) from those of kind-membership and essentialism; only in the latter two cases does Locke have an axe to grind. In the end, we shall see that nothing in Locke's text suggests that he need deny that there are objective, particularized properties of objects at the corpuscular level that explain their resemblance in a given respect. What he wishes to deny is that these properties compel or justify our decision to select some and not others as essential for kind-membership. Nevertheless, any such decision is not arbitrary and can be evaluated in terms of its ability to map at least *some* of the objective resemblances and in terms of its practical value. What we find, then, is that Locke offers an appealing mixture of realism and anti-realism on these issues.

ABSTRACTION

Like most everything else in Locke's philosophy, the discussion of abstraction is notoriously difficult to interpret. I shall argue, *pace* the current trend in the scholarship, that Locke conceives of abstraction as mental separation. Although Locke requires selective attention for abstraction, it is not to be identified with abstraction itself.

Locke uses abstract ideas in two ways: as standards or patterns that things might fit or fail to fit, and as representations of a class of particulars.[2] They account not only for our ability to think about classes of things, but also for the truth and falsity of statements of the form "x is F (where F is a property) or an F (where F is a sortal term)." This is to be determined, as we shall see below, by checking to see whether x "agrees with" the abstract idea of F (or an F). Since Locke's concern with language focuses on precisely these categorical statements, much will turn on his ability to provide an intelligible analysis of them capable of supplanting the Aristotelian view. Such an analysis would determine the truth of statements such as the one above by checking the relation between substantial form and property, in the paradigmatic case. (The Aristotelian view is developed at greater length in the next chapter.)

[2] Ayers (1991, vol. 1, p. 248).

In addition to explaining our ability to think of simple qualities, abstract ideas are also supposed to explain how we can think about classes of things. Locke must posit both simple and complex abstract ideas, since they must range over not only simple qualities (such as whiteness), but substances such as human beings. Although, as I shall argue, the process by which both of these ideas are generated is properly called a kind of mental separation, this belies some significant differences between them.

Before considering particular texts in detail, I wish to set out three central problems that any defensible account of Lockean abstraction must be able to answer.

(1) Locke says in numerous places that abstraction consists in separating simple ideas from complex ones (see, e.g., III.iii.9). But Locke is equally clear that all ideas enter the senses "simple and unmixed" (II.i.1: 119). What need is there, then, for such separation?[3]

(2) In abstraction, the mind "make[s] nothing new, but only leave[s] out of the complex *Idea* [of the particular instances] that which is peculiar to each, and retain[s] only what is common to all" (III.iii.7: 411). Although this might seem plausible in the case of simple ideas, it is much harder to see how it can be true of complex abstract ideas. Locke seems committed to the principle that the senses afford us awareness only of fully determinate features. But if this is so, how can a single idea range over a number of particulars, which might not share *any* determinate features? An abstract idea of mankind that includes a fully determinate set of facial features or even number of limbs would be wholly inadequate to representing every individual falling under the sortal term "mankind." So it seems that the mind must in some sense "make something new," insofar as the abstract idea must include determinable, not determinate, features.

(3) Locke claims that generality is only a relation ideas are placed in; intrinsically, nothing at all is general (III.iii.11; examined below). If this is true, it is hard to see why Locke needs to posit abstract ideas at all. Abstract ideas would be perfectly ordinary and fully determinate ideas plucked from the chorus to serve as representations of a given kind. (Indeed, most of my opponents, who claim that Lockean abstraction is selective attention rather than mental separation, point to this passage for support.) But the claim that generality is a wholly extrinsic relation sits uneasily with other of Locke's commitments. What, then, is Locke's real position? Or is he simply inconsistent?

---

[3] Willis Doney raises this issue; see his (1956).

We can make a start on this last question by examining Locke's account of knowledge and working back to the mechanisms of abstraction.[4] We have seen that "proposition" is ambiguous for Locke between mental and verbal propositions; the latter are parasitic on the former, so it is with mental propositions that we are concerned. Thus S can be said to know that φ (a mental proposition) when S sees that the ideas composing φ agree or disagree, depending upon whether φ contains sub-propositional affirmation or negation and whether the ideas of φ do in fact so agree or disagree. This model works best in evaluating definitions: is man a rational animal? That depends upon whether those two ideas are included in one's idea of man. Locke is quite clear in saying that knowledge can never extend beyond one's own ideas, strictly speaking, although when these ideas in turn represent real objects outside the mind, it can be said to know true propositions about them. Locke writes,

Every Man's Reasoning and Knowledge, is only about the *Ideas* existing in his own Mind, which are truly, every one of them, particular Existences: and our Knowledge and Reasoning about other Things, is only as they correspond with those our particular *Ideas*. So that the Perception of the Agreement, or Disagreement of our particular *Ideas*, is the whole and utmost of all our Knowledge. Universality is but accidental to it, and consists only in this, That the particular *Ideas*, about which it is, are such, as more than one particular Thing can correspond with, and be represented by. (IV.xvii.8: 680–1)

In what sense is universality "accidental" to knowledge? Locke is adamant that only particulars exist; but then how is universality to be achieved at all? Locke does seem, at the end of the passage, to posit an intrinsic generality to some ideas insofar as they are such as multiple things can be represented by. What makes them suited for this work, and how is this consistent with Locke's consistent disavowal of intrinsic generality?

Given that ideas are the ineliminable intermediary between mind and world, our knowledge can be said to reach beyond our ideas only when they succeed in representing extra-mental things. This lets us see why Locke claims that universality is "accidental" to knowledge: our ideas themselves are particular, but when they range over a number of other particulars, they can be said to be universal, and our knowledge with them. This universality is not a property of the ideas themselves; it consists in the *relation* of agreement between the idea and other particulars. Nevertheless, the ideas in question must have the intrinsic property of being able to

---

[4] This strategy is suggested by Ayers (1997).

represent particulars. And as I shall argue below, their universality consists partly in the use to which we put them.

With this in mind, let us turn to III.iii.11, the centerpiece of my opponents' arguments:

Ideas are general, when they are set up, as the Representatives of many particular Things: but universality belongs not to things themselves, which are all of them particular in their Existence, even those Words, and *Ideas*, which, in their signification are general. (III.iii.11: 414)

Universality, then, is not an intrinsic character of anything, whether a physical object or an idea. Ideas are general, that is, they apply to more than one thing, when we craft them in such a way that they represent many particulars. We must distinguish between the properties of the idea (e.g., it exists in a mind, it is thought of at this moment, or what have you) from the properties the idea *represents*. An idea as a mental object is always fully determinate and particular. But what it represents need not be. There is in general no inference from the properties of a representation to those of what is represented. Ideas are not themselves universal or general (allowing that Locke uses these terms interchangeably) even though there is no bar to their having a content that applies to many individuals. Locke continues:

When therefore we quit Particulars, the Generals that rest, are only Creatures of our own making, their general Nature being nothing but the Capacity they are put into by the Understanding, of signifying or representing many particulars. For the signification they have, is nothing but a relation, that by the Mind of Man is added to them.

Locke appears to be claiming that there is nothing about the idea itself that explains its generality. But this cannot be his position, or so I shall argue, since he posits abstraction as a process issuing in an idea whose content, while present in the initial idea(s) from which it was generated, must be separated from the other ideas with which it was presented in experience. The generality, then, must have a foundation in the intrinsic character of the idea's intentional object: if an idea represents dogs, its content must in some way "conform" to dogs. Locke's point is, first, that the general nature is a function of the content of the idea rather than of any feature the idea *qua* mental item possesses, and second, that the abstract idea must have a particular causal history: it must have been made by its owner in order to represent what it does in fact represent. Given Locke's denial of innate ideas, any abstract idea will have this history. If, perhaps *per impossibile*, an idea of a determinable arrangement of neutrinos were suddenly to pop into my head, it would not for me be a representation of that arrangement of neutrinos, but simply a very odd mental flash. This is the relation added by the mind of man: the idea has been formed on the basis of experience for the purpose of representing individuals.

With this as background, let us turn to the first kind of abstraction Locke must posit, which involves simple qualities. In constructing an abstract idea of white, for instance, the mind does not need to combine previous ideas or drain them of any content, but only to separate them. The central issue concerns what this separation amounts to. Most commentators suggest that Locke appeals to a process of selective attention, whereby the mind attends to some features of a single idea and ignores others. If this is right, then Locke must deny what Kenneth Winkler has called the "content assumption": the assumption that the content of thought is fixed by the idea. The mind would generate an abstract idea of white not by separating it from the other ideas with which it was initially bundled in sensation but by holding a complex idea and attending to some aspect, in this case the color, and neglecting others. Commentators such as C.C.W. Taylor, J.L. Mackie, Michael Ayers and Winkler all hold that Locke not only endorses the selective attention model but that it is his *only* model for understanding abstraction. But I shall show that the text normally appealed to in order to justify this reading is insufficient. Instead, Locke holds that one gains an idea of white, for example, by separating it from its concomitant ideas. This presupposes selective attention in that before one can separate idea A from ideas B and C one must first have the complex idea ABC and selectively attend to A before one is in a position to separate A from ABC. So abstraction, on my view, requires but is not identical with selective attention. In the case of complex ideas of substances, Locke seems to require an idea of a determinable in order to represent things falling under a given sortal term. I shall argue that the standard objections to this reading of Locke are inadequate. At most, they show that Locke's commitment to abstraction in this sense is in tension with his position on conceivability and possibility. But even this tension disappears, or so I shall argue, once one sees the passages in question in their proper context.[5]

According to Locke, the third power of the mind is "separating them [ideas] from all other *Ideas* that accompany them in their real existence; this is called *Abstraction*" (II.xii.1: 163). On its face, this is an unambiguous endorsement of the separation model. My opponents, however, typically point to Locke's discussion of abstraction in the previous chapter. In II.xi.9:

---

[5] Other commentators who have argued against the dominant view of Lockean abstraction include Christopher Panza (forthcoming) and Jonathan Walmsley (1999). I am indebted to their work in what follows, with the exception of my treatment of space.

159, Locke writes, "the Mind makes the particular *Ideas*, received from particular Objects, to become general; which is done by considering them as they are in the Mind such Appearances, separate from all other Existences, and the circumstances of real Existence, as Time, Place, or any other concomitant *Ideas*." It is not immediately clear that this amounts to selective attention, as Winkler and others have assumed. For in order to generate an abstract idea, one considers it *apart from* its concomitant ideas, which Locke thinks are distinct from it. So it is not that there is a *single* idea before the mind that includes the circumstances of real existence Locke lists. Instead, this passage suggests that there are multiple ideas, only one of which is before the mind after the process of abstraction has been completed. This, of course, is compatible with the content assumption. Later in the passage, however, Locke writes, "the same Colour being observed to day in Chalk or Snow, which the mind yesterday received from Milk, it considers that Appearance alone, makes it a representative of all that kind" (II.xi.9: 159). But this still does not amount to a clear endorsement of the selective attention model, since of course one way to consider the appearance alone is simply to think about the simple idea of white without thinking of the ideas with which it came into the senses.[6] The quick inference to selective attention depends on conflating these distinct ideas into one, whereas Locke, of course, holds that the ideas provided by experience are all *simple* ideas (see, e.g., II.i.1: 119). (I shall have more to say about this when I discuss problem (2) below.)

If we are committed to reading Locke literally where possible, as I believe we should be, we must take his consistent talk of abstraction as separation seriously. On my reading, abstraction in this sense amounts to thinking of an idea without thinking of its concomitant ideas. This is distinct from attending to some aspect of an idea and not others. At this point we need to examine Locke's discussion of space (II.xiii.13), the text Winkler cites as "decisive" in favor of attributing to Locke only the selective attention model. In this passage, Locke wishes to distinguish what he calls partial consideration from mental division. Locke seems to argue that the parts of space are indivisible even in thought because they cannot be divided in reality. Although Winkler takes this to mean that "Locke, like Berkeley, is unwilling to allow mental separation where he refuses to allow actual separation,"[7] this is far from obvious. For there might be considerations particular to the idea of space that make such separation impossible. What

---

[6] C.C.W. Taylor (1978) also recognizes that these passages are ambiguous between the two models of abstraction in question.

[7] Winkler (1989, p. 41).

is more important, I shall argue that in these passages Locke is not speaking of separation in the sense required by abstraction. Instead, he speaks of "mental Separation, or Division" (II.xiii.13: 172). It will emerge that there is a subtle but important difference between the separation involved in abstraction and mental division.

We must begin by noting that these passages about space are not presented in the course of a discussion of abstraction and are certainly not presented by Locke as an account of that process. Nowhere does Locke connect these considerations about space with abstraction. Locke's aim is to show that body and extension are distinct *ideas* (II.xiii.11: 171); to do so he points to a number of properties included in the one concept but not the other. Among these is the property of divisibility: bodies are clearly divisible, but space itself, with which Descartes had identified extension, is not. Space is a simple idea which we get through sight and touch (II.xiii.2: 167), whereas its modes are complex ideas which "contain not in them the supposition of subsisting by themselves, but are considered as Dependencies on, or Affections of, Substances" (II.xii.4: 165). Thus Locke seems to begin by treating space as a substance on which modes depend, though later in II.xiii he will raise the question whether space is indeed a substance or an accident.

What is important for my opponents, especially Ayers and Winkler, is the general prohibition they think II.xiii contains against mental separation without the possibility of physical separation. Winkler, for example, reads Locke as committing himself to the more general Berkeleyan thesis that conceivability entails possibility, the contrapositive of which would prohibit abstract ideas. If it is impossible for what an idea represents to exist, and this certainly seems to be the case at least with abstract ideas of kinds, then the idea in question is similarly impossible. The solution offered by these commentators is that Locke, like Berkeley, conceives of abstraction only as selective attention.

As I shall show, however, this position is not supported by the text. The passages in question show Locke issuing a prohibition against mental *division*, not mental abstraction *qua* separation, and that only in the case of space. Abstraction and division are distinguished by the fact that the latter involves a further act of the mind over and above holding before the mind a simple idea that has been split off from another. This is obscured by Locke's loose usage of "divide" and "separate"; but the substance of what he says will make clear that there is in fact an important difference between these, even if in the context of the passage under consideration he was not concerned to draw this distinction explicitly. That there is a distinction is signaled by the fact that the passages concerning abstraction speak of separation only, never division.

Here is the beginning of Locke's passage:

To divide and separate actually, is, as I think, by removing the parts from one another, to make two Superficies [surfaces], where before there was a Continuity: And to divide mentally, is to make in the Mind two Superficies, where before there was a Continuity, and *consider them as removed one from the other*; which can only be done in things considered by the Mind, as capable of being separated . . . (II.xiii.13: 172; italics mine).

To divide the parts of space mentally, then, involves more than simply holding in mind an idea of a part of space that was formerly contained in another idea of a part of space. What is said to be impossible is only doing so when at the same time considering the two ideas as removed from one another. Mental division is *not* abstraction, for abstraction involves forming an idea of a quality or class of things by distilling some element already present in the idea(s) given in the senses; division contains an extra mental act. Locke argues that division is not possible in the mind where it is not possible in reality, but this by itself does not rule out abstraction in my sense.

'Tis true, a Man may consider so much of such a *Space*, as is answerable or commensurate to a Foot, without considering the rest; which is indeed a par-tial Consideration, but not so much as mental Separation, or Division; since a Man can no more mentally divide, *without considering two Superficies, separate one from the other*, than he can actually divide, without making two Superficies dis-join'd one from the other: But a partial consideration is not separating. A Man may consider Light in the Sun, without its heat; or Mobility in Body without its extension, without thinking of their separation. One is only a partial considera-tion, terminating in one alone; and the other is a Consideration of both, as existing separately. (II.xiii.13: 172–3; second emphasis mine)

As in the earlier texts, it is simply not clear whether "partial consideration" is to be identified with mental separation as I have defined it or with selective attention. For surely one way to think of light in the sun without thinking of its being separate from the sun is simply to have before the mind an idea of light that one has separated from the other constituent ideas of the complex idea of the sun. This reading is supported by the last line of the quoted passage: partial consideration "terminates" in one surface (or idea of that surface), not in a consideration of an aspect of that surface or idea.

However that may be, it is clear that both of these processes are to be contrasted with mental division, which involves thinking of *two* surfaces

("Superficies") as existing separately or as divided. In order for an act of thought to violate Locke's principle that one can no more mentally divide space than one can physically divide it, it would have to include a thought of two surfaces *as existing separately*. But simply thinking of a single idea of a part of space does not include this. It is only when one adds that there is another part of space distinct from it that the problem is generated. There is no suggestion in the text that this predicament is widespread; in fact, it seems to turn on features peculiar to space. Commentators have consistently missed the fact that mental division is here defined specifically as it relates to space: there is obviously no suggestion on Locke's part that we achieve abstract ideas by "mak[ing] two Superficies, where before there was a Continuity."

What is it about pure space that makes it incapable of mental division? The only way to divide something mentally is to think of an idea of a continuity and thus in thought make two surfaces; then one must make the further judgment that the two are removed from one another. But in the case of space itself, there is no way to do this, for in introducing distinct surfaces, we are thinking of separating only body, not space itself.[8]

Although it makes sense to speak of dividing or moving body, the same cannot be said of extension or space. Thus, *contra* Descartes, extension and body are two distinct ideas, which was exactly what Locke set out to prove. None of this has any bearing on the very different matter of separating a simple idea out of a complex one. Contrast the genesis of the abstract idea of white. In this case, we split this idea off from the other constituents of the complex idea. There is no reason to suppose that here, as in the case of parts of space, we must also divide these ideas, which here would involve affirming that the quality white and the other qualities which make up the complex source idea represent independent objects.

Locke's discussion of space, then, is by no means in tension with his earlier pronouncement (II.xii.1, examined above) that abstraction is mental separation. Nor is any difficulty created by Locke's arguing that there is no necessary connection between space and solidity on purely conceptual grounds.[9] For Locke is arguing in II.xiii for a distinction between the *ideas* of body and extension/space, a point Winkler and others consistently miss. True enough, there is an important upshot to all of this: Locke argues that if we knew the real essence of body to be extension, our ideas of both would

---

[8] Thus Jonathan Walmsley writes, "The parts of pure space, then, cannot be separated from each other, as any such separation would involve the introduction of body, and such an introduction would mean that we are not now thinking of pure space" (1999, p. 132).

[9] Winkler (1989, p. 41).

be the same, so that we could never go wrong in substituting one word for the other.[10] All of this is rather far from the problem of abstraction.

There are independent grounds for thinking that Locke does not endorse Winkler's conceivability principle. If Locke did hold this principle, he would either be inconsistent or else we would have to read away most of his official claims about abstraction. For Locke is quite clear in saying that an indeterminate triangle, for example, "is something imperfect, that cannot exist" (IV.vii.9: 596). Locke is not saying, of course, that the *idea* is impossible. Although the idea of a determinable triangle serves to represent triangles, nothing that is merely determinable can exist in reality, even if it *can* exist in the mind in the sense that an idea can have it as its immediate intentional object. Locke must therefore distinguish between nomological and logical impossibility: determinable triangles are not logically inconsistent but prohibited from existing outside the mind, presumably by the laws of nature. Winkler, of course, denies that Locke has the resources to make such a distinction. Indeed, the conceivability principle depends on eliding any such distinction, and Berkeley cheerfully accepts the consequence that only self-contradictory things or states of affairs can be said to be impossible. Although Winkler argues that the moderns in general do not distinguish different kinds of modality, with the result that possibility collapses into *logical* possibility alone, this is debatable. Michael Ayers, for example, argues that Locke has room for synthetic *a priori* laws.[11] In these cases, the possibility of a thing or event would be determined not by logical consistency, but by whether or not they violate these laws. But I do not wish to insist upon this point. It seems to me far more clear simply to point to the notorious triangle passage for a distinction between logical and nomological possibility. Obviously Locke is not saying that the abstract idea itself is impossible; nor does he think that particular triangles are impossible; he must then think that the determinable triangle, what we might call the content of the idea, is impossible. But clearly it is not *logically* impossible, like a square circle; if it were, it would also be inconceivable. Instead, it violates the laws of nature: no physical thing can exist that is not fully determinate in every respect.

To support his attribution of the conceivability principle to Locke, Winkler adverts to IV.iii.6, where Locke claims that it is possible for thought to be annexed to matter because he can "see no contradiction in it." But of course this makes only for epistemic possibility: as far as I

---

[10] Ayers calls this the "argument from language" (1991, vol. 2, pp. 51–64). See below, chapter four.
[11] For such a distinction in Locke, see IV.viii.8; see Ayers (1991, vol. 2., ch. 12).

can tell, Goldbach's conjecture might be true, because I cannot detect a contradiction. But there is a clear gap between our being unable at this moment to detect a contradiction and one's really being present.

Let us see how this reading of the first kind of abstraction fares when set against the remaining two problems outlined above. The first problem asked why, since sensation only provides simple ideas, there is any need for abstraction. Why couldn't the mind simply focus on one of these ideas? To see why abstraction is necessary, we must look at Locke's account of substances.

The Mind being, as I have declared, furnished with a great number of simple *Ideas*, conveyed by the *Senses*, as they are found in exterior things, or by *Reflection* on its own Operations, takes notice also, that a certain number of these simple *Ideas* go constantly together; which being presumed to belong to one thing, and Words being suited to common apprehensions, and made use of for quick despatch, are called so united in one subject, by one name; which by inadvertancy we are apt afterward to talk of and consider as one simple *Idea*, which indeed is a complication of many *Ideas* together . . . (II.xxiii.1: 295)

Although it is true that only simple ideas are available in experience, the mind is disposed to assume that the variety of simple ideas received on a certain occasion is in fact a *single* simple idea. So even though in experience we perceive simple ideas, we tend to lump those ideas that "go constantly together" into a single complex idea; it then takes effort to separate out the original constituent ideas. Upon reflection, Locke thinks we will see that our ideas of substances (such as man, horse, etc.) are complex rather than simple. He does not, however, think that this fact is immediately obvious in introspection.

The second and final remaining problem asks how it is that the mind can be said to "make nothing new" when it generates an abstract idea. But in the present case the answer is clear enough: the content of the abstract idea of a quality is itself contained in that of the complex idea of a substance. Thus in order to think of that quality, one need only separate it from the others.

Thus, whether by selective attention or by separation, Locke clearly holds that we are able to form general ideas of qualities on the basis of experience. These ideas are given in experience and require only to have the ideas with which they were initially experienced amputated, as it were, in order to become general. We are now in a position to turn to complex, rather than simple, abstract ideas, which can represent kinds of substances. This case is the more difficult, as it involves the formation of ideas of whose intentional objects are not given, or at least not given as such, in experience. How is one to form the idea of a human being on the basis of the individual humans one has seen? Even if one were to strip away the determining features of time and place, one would still be left with an idea of a particular human.

The famous passages in Book III suggest the following picture: after observing several individuals, one forms a general idea, wherein one "make[s] nothing new, but only leave[s] out of the complex *Idea* [of the particular instances] that which is peculiar to each, and retain[s] only what is common to all" (III.iii.7: 411). On Locke's view, we must construct a new idea by draining away some content from the initial one. The idea then becomes general in virtue of being an idea *of* a determinable. For example, the idea of human being must include the property of having some height or other, but not any height will do (a humanoid form that stood ten miles high would not match up with most of our ideas of human being).

Is it possible to have an idea that is an idea of a determinable in the requisite sense? If abstract ideas are construed as images, the answer must be yes. There are two relevant kinds of indeterminacy. First, there is the obvious sense in which an image as it were has nothing to say on a certain issue. Does Goya's Colossus have an ingrown toenail? Does he have a scar on the right side of his face? The painting says nothing one way or another. Second, and more problematically perhaps, images can have content that is itself indeterminate and not merely that leaves some questions open. For example, if one forms an image of a tiger, is it necessary that the *image* have a fully determinate number of stripes? Tigers, of course, must be fully determinate in every respect; but this does not prevent mental images from being indeterminate.

Even if we grant all of this, however, we must acknowledge that Locke's account of abstraction does not fit very neatly with his account of representation (see above, chapter 1). Recall that simple ideas represent in virtue of their causal and teleological connections with their objects. This works well if we restrict ourselves to the abstraction of simple ideas. In such cases, we separate off a single idea that has its representational powers as it were built in: once we separate it off from the other ideas with which it was intromitted by the senses, the simple idea of white represents the relevant quality (type, and not just token) in the object that caused that idea. But what can Locke say about *complex* abstract ideas, such as the idea of a horse? Here, in sharp contrast to his discussion of simple ideas of sensation, he relies on resemblance. But between what sorts of things is the resemblance supposed to hold? If between an idea and the real object, the resemblance would obtain only with regard to ideas of primary qualities. But clearly most of our substance ideas will also involve ideas of secondary qualities as well, primarily color, but also, in some cases, taste and the other secondary qualities (see II.xxxi.8: 381). In such cases, the resemblance relation will not hold.

Need we read Locke as committing himself to this account of resemblance with regard to complex abstract ideas? Let me suggest another way, equally consistent with the texts, in which to make sense of Locke's view. One forms these ideas by noting resemblances among particulars and omitting those features in which the particulars diverge. It is natural to say, then, that one recognizes x as of type y when one's *idea* of x (and not x itself) resembles y in the relevant respects. Thus, the resemblance that funds the representational capabilities of complex abstract ideas obtains between the complex, fully particular idea we get from sensation and another idea, viz., the abstract idea. Even if ideas of secondary qualities cannot resemble anything *in the objects themselves*, they can surely resemble one another.

This reading seems justified in light of Locke's remarks in II.xxx and II.xxxi. The reality and adequacy of complex ideas of substances depends not on the degree to which they resemble the objects they represent but rather on the degree to which they capture the co-existence in experience of the simple ideas that make them up. Locke writes that complex ideas of substances "are no farther *real*, than as they are Combinations of simple *Ideas*, as are really united, and co-exist in Things without us" (II.xxx.5: 374). Here Locke's self-consciously ambiguous use of "idea" (see II.viii.8: 134) complicates matters. Locke surely does not mean that the ideas really exist in extra-mental things. If we compare a later passage, Locke's meaning becomes a bit clearer. Locke says that our ideas of substances are inadequate, for "whatever Collection of simple *Ideas* it makes of any Substance that exists, [the mind] cannot be sure, that it exactly answers all that are in the Substance" (II.xxxi.13: 383). When forming our ideas of substances, our aim, in the usual case, is to include all and only those simple ideas whose co-existence has been experienced. Given the way simple ideas represent, the idea/quality ambiguity is virtuous: the presence of a simple idea in experience indicates the corresponding presence of the quality that produces it. The barriers to adequacy and reality arise when we try to discern the purely accidental co-occurrences of such qualities from those that are not. In terms of representation, however, the resemblance relation that allows a complex abstract idea to be applied to a number of particular substances obtains not between the idea and those substances but between the abstract idea and the *ideas* of those substances. It is then a further question whether the qualities that the simple ideas represent are "really united" in the extra-mental object or have occurred together for some other reason.

If I am right, it is not strictly accurate to cast Locke as a purely causal (or causal-cum-teleological) theorist with regard to representation. He must invoke resemblance to explain representation at the level of complex abstract ideas; the resemblance holds between two ideas, and not an idea and its extra-mental object. If it is difficult to see how a mental object could resemble something extra-mental, it should be correspondingly easier to see how two mental objects might resemble each other. The difficulties, however, with making resemblance do *any* of the work of representation are so well known I shall not go through them here.[12] It is worth pointing out that Locke's failed attempt to account for the representation of complex ideas makes him no worse off than contemporary theorists who attempt similar reductions of representation. For one of the most serious difficulties afflicting the projects of Fodor, Dretske, Millikan, and others, is their apparent inability to explain how complex concepts and mental states are generated. The point retains its force even though "simple" and "complex" obviously mean different things in Lockean and contemporary contexts. It is one thing to explain the content of a mental state such as the belief that it is raining; it is quite another to explain the content of mental states that are far removed from the context of indication, or that of any of the other recently proposed naturalistic analyses.[13] For our purposes, it is enough to see that Locke's two-tiered approach to representation allows him to acknowledge the role of the mind in forming abstract ideas of kinds while still anchoring the representation of simple ideas to their (proper) causes.

Having addressed objections (1) and (3) above, we are now in a position to deal with (2), which presents a genuine problem for abstract ideas in this second sense only. (2) asks how Locke can posit a process or method by which abstract ideas are created and at the same time hold that in creating such ideas the mind "makes nothing new." It seems that the content of any abstract idea must in some sense already be present in experience. Although this posed no problems for abstract ideas of qualities, it remains obscure how experience could contain the determinable features requisite for abstract ideas of kinds. I think there is a perfectly good sense in which forming an idea of a determinable from determinates can be said to introduce no new features. For what made the idea a representation of a particular in the first place was the determinacy of its content in the relevant respects: the idea represented, say, a Peruvian hairless rather than dogs-in-general.

---

[12] For a brief discussion of the problems with resemblance as representation, see Cummins (1989, p. 46).

[13] See Crane (1995, p. 189).

It makes sense for Locke to say that abstraction is a process of omitting irrelevant details while retaining the feature of dog-in-general, which the content of the original idea also had. But the problem is not to be brushed off so quickly. The sense in which the original content can be said to have this feature seems attenuated at best: it did not represent dogs-in-general but only those of the Peruvian hairless breed. There are at least two interpretative options: we can say that Locke did not mean his claim that the mind makes nothing new when it makes abstract ideas to be taken in the way I have taken it, or we can say that experience itself reveals determinable features.[14] Neither option is attractive, but the latter may seem preferable if we consider that a determinate feature may "contain" a determinable in the sense that it contains the *material* for forming the idea of the determinable. That is, the idea's features are such that performing the appropriate abstractive process on it is sufficient to produce the relevant abstract idea.

OBJECTIONS AND REPLIES

In this section I shall consider briefly what I take to be the two most prominent objections to Locke's view. It is important to see that this inquiry is distinct from the interpretative project of the previous section. However well or badly a given view fares is not in general relevant to the issue of whether a philosopher holds that view. Nevertheless, it is worth noting that Locke's account as I have interpreted it has the resources to answer these objections.

The first objection, presented by Wittgenstein in the *Blue and Brown Books* and leveled against Locke by Bennett, argues that Locke's account presupposes the very ability it is supposed to explain.[15] For classifying *ideas* seems no different in kind from classifying *things*. Consider, for example, the account Locke would give of someone recognizing an animal as an aardvark. One is presented with a visual image of the creature and then consults one's catalogue of abstract ideas to find one that fits the image. But how is it that, although I could not simply look at the aardvark and recognize it, I can "look" at my abstract idea of an aardvark and recognize *it*? The abstract ideas which determine what kind of thing a particular item is are themselves particulars, no less in need of classification than extra-mental objects.

[14] I am indebted to Christopher Panza for making me see this difficulty.
[15] See Wittgenstein (1958, p. 3) and Bennett (1971, p. 15).

The objection needs to be developed a bit more carefully if it is to apply to Locke, however. For Locke, the issue cannot be how we recognize aardvarks, since his representationalism entails that we perceive aardvarks only through the mediation of our ideas. It is the idea given in sensation, not the thing the idea represents, that needs classifying. If for the moment we assume that Lockean ideas are images, the "matching" of a new idea to an abstract idea becomes more perspicuous. Locke might well have conceived this process as the mental analogue of sliding a piece of tracing paper over a number of other drawings in order to see which one it matched.

This conception of recognition fits neatly with E.J. Lowe's rejoinder to the Wittgensteinian argument. Locke's view is indeed in peril if he held that our abstract ideas themselves stand in need of classification. But Locke might reply that the mechanism by which one applies an abstract idea to a new item of experience is automatic, in the way that a vending machine's "recognition" of a quarter is automatic. Matching the idea of the aardvark with the appropriate abstract idea does not require an extra step whereby one recognizes that the abstract idea is an idea of an aardvark.[16] To Lowe's proposal, however, the Wittgensteinian will reply that if automatic processes are to be invoked in the case of abstract ideas, why could they not be invoked at the initial stage, when one is first presented with the novel item of experience? This would circumvent the need for abstract ideas altogether. The challenge to Locke is to show a difference in kind between the recognition of ideas of sensation and that of abstract ideas; there is no reason to think that abstract ideas "wear their character on their faces," as it were, while ideas given in sensation do not.

This reply in fact reveals the central weakness of the Wittgensteinian argument. For what exactly is it to "classify an abstract idea?" We know what it is to classify an idea of sensation: it is to determine that it agrees with or fits a certain abstract idea. But what then is left to explain? Perhaps the Wittgensteinian is asking for an account of why we associate a given word with an abstract idea. "Classifying" the abstract idea, then, would be determining which word signifies that idea. But this is a demand that Locke can meet. Let us back up a moment and consider very briefly Locke's account of language learning. When first learning the signification of a categorematic word, one might need to be given an ostensive definition, or a definition in terms of other words.[17] After this instruction has "taken," a causal connection is set up whereby hearing a given word causes one to

---

[16] See Lowe (1995, p. 165).
[17] Wittgenstein, of course, challenges ostensive definition as means of linguistic instruction. I consider this below; see chapter six.

have the associated idea. Why shouldn't the connection go the other way as well? Locke might well hold that having a certain abstract idea brings to mind the idea of the word associated with it. There is no need for a further process of recognition to determine which word is associated with a given abstract idea.

The second common objection stems from the work of Peter Geach.[18] On Locke's view, we must (at least at some early stage of our mental development) be able to identify and re-identify objects without bringing them under concepts. Concept formation is posterior to our experience of a world of objects. But how is it that we can individuate objects before applying concepts to them? How can we think of the aardvark as a distinct item in need of classification without thinking of it *as* an animal, or a living thing, or what have you? Locke seems to require that we can fix our attention on objects without applying any sortal terms to them at all.

To answer this objection, it is not necessary to make the ontological claim that the world is sorted into discrete objects and then work back to our apprehension of this fact. Indeed, it is one of Locke's central claims that our pre-theoretical conception of the world is in many respects mistaken. What Locke needs is some way to account for the origin of this pre-theoretical conception in the first place. Locke seems to take for granted that we do in fact individuate objects prior to having an abstract idea that would allow us to think of them as members of a certain kind. A natural account for him to give of this process is to posit a psychological disposition to individuate objects as we do. It seems true that some ways of "carving up" the world are more natural to us than others. Locke can accept the point made by contemporary empiricists such as Quine and Goodman that this naturalness does not reflect anything in the nature of the things themselves. Our tendency to think of a rabbit, for instance, as a distinct object from the grass on which it sits might well have a basis in evolutionary psychology. To adapt a phrase of Quine's, creatures who do not individuate animals from their settings, for example, have the pathetic but praiseworthy habit of dying out.

To what extent does this answer the objection? Once again we see Locke driven to posit an automatic psychological mechanism. The natural reply is that this is inconsistent with his empiricism.[19] After all, Locke inveighs against innate ideas; how then can he help himself to these innate mechanisms? But the claim that human beings are predisposed to sort the things

---

[18] See Geach (1957, §§6–11).
[19] Lowe (1995, p. 163) makes a parallel point about the detection of resemblance, an issue treated above.

they encounter in one way rather than another is in no way inconsistent with the denial of innate ideas. What would be innate is not an idea at all but rather a capacity. Even the most rabid empiricist must, after all, grant that some capacities are innate in human beings. Locke does not claim that the pre-theoretical picture of the world generated with the help of these capacities mirrors anything in nature. Moreover, Locke's famous character-ization of the mind as a "tabula rasa" must be balanced against his claim that the mind at birth is an "empty Cabinet" (I.ii.15: 55). The metaphors are importantly different, since, unlike a blank slate, a cabinet has some structure. Locke might well have thought that this structure was the result of innate psychological mechanisms.

I have done no more in this section than sketch some replies Locke might make to these familiar objections. I propose now to consider his position on the related topics of properties and universals.

REALISM AND NOMINALISM

Locke's account of abstraction, as I have said, is meant to function as a replacement for the Aristotelian account of intentionality, especially where natural kinds are concerned. Although it is usual to subsume the question of natural kinds under that of properties or universals, Locke's novel move is to give a quite different treatment to each. Since his main purpose is to attack the Aristotelians, he spends most of his time arguing against realism about natural kinds. Falling under a kind is simply agreeing with a nominal essence, which itself is an abstract idea. Thus Locke's positive position on natural kinds is naturally much more perspicuous than his position on properties; nevertheless, the outlines of his position can be discerned. We should not be misled, however, into thinking that the two questions are totally independent of one another. R.I. Aaron, for example, makes this mistake when he writes, "Locke might have denied that we knew real essences in the case of species and genera and yet have affirmed that we knew universals in the realist sense in the case of universals of quality. But he never considers these points."[20] In the course of his anti-Aristotelian arguments, Locke, as we have seen, claims that everything that exists is particular; there are thus no universals of quality out there to know. But Aaron is right to point out that conceptual nominalism at the level of natural kinds does not imply a similar nominalism about qualities or properties.

[20] Aaron (1952, p. 40).

What complicates matters here is that the term "nominalist" can refer to a wide array of positions. For if Locke is a nominalist in the sense that he believes that everything is particular, so too, arguably, are Aristotle and perhaps even Plato. (After all, if we take seriously Plato's position in the *Timaeus* that the forms are exemplars, it seems they must themselves be particular.) To be more precise, I propose to use the term instead to refer to those views that hold that there is no mind- or language-independent justification for grouping things or qualities under a single heading. Even within this camp, we can distinguish the restricted nominalist, who imposes extra-linguistic or extra-mental limits on the nature and number of kinds we construct, from what we might pejoratively call the rabid nominalist, who accepts no such constraints. (The latter view is extremely unpopular, although certain of Hobbes's remarks lead one to believe that he was sympathetic to it.) In this sense, I shall argue, Locke is a restricted nominalist with regard to natural kinds, but a realist with regard to properties construed as foundations of objective resemblances at the corpuscular level.

Locke tells us that nominal essences are the abstract ideas signified by general terms. At both the micro- and macro-physical levels, Locke holds that there are objective resemblances. "Nature, in the Production of Things, makes several of them alike"; sorting things under names "*is the Workmanship of the Understanding, taking occasion from the similitude* it observes amongst them" (III.iii.13: 415). Locke's version of concept nominalism, then, falls into the category of "restricted" nominalism, set out above. In addition to pragmatic constraints on our groupings of things, Locke recognizes constraints imposed by objective resemblances. The crucial departure from realism that Locke effects turns on the claim that objective resemblance does not uniquely determine a particular classification or sorting of the objects in question. So although we must be responsive to these resemblances, we cannot suppose that they justify us in choosing one system of concepts over another. We are always free to ask why this particular point of resemblance should be chosen over another in constructing our idea of a kind.

Nevertheless, Locke's doctrine of real essences might seem to take the bite out of his nominalism. For his picture might seem to suggest that we are justified in positing a single real essence isomorphic to each nominal essence. That Locke does not hold this is clear. For one of his key arguments against the claim that nominal rather than real essences determine kind-membership for us turns on the claim that members of the same kind often exhibit different properties. Locke writes,

That we find many of the Individuals that are ranked into one Sort, called by one common Name, and so received as being of one *Species*, have yet Qualities depending on their real Constitutions, as far different one from another, as from others, from which they are accounted to differ *specifically*. This, as it is easy to be observed by all, who have to do with natural Bodies; so Chymists especially are often, by sad Experience, convinced of it, when they, sometimes in vain, seek for the same Qualities in one parcel of Sulphur, Antinomy, or Vitriol, which they have found in others. (III.vi.8: 443)

The pre-theoretical sorting of objects according to their readily observable properties is obviously subject to correction.[21] What is of interest here is the suggestion that so long as we cannot penetrate to the real essences of things, there is always the chance that the objective resemblances at the macro-physical level are explained not by the persistence of a single real essence or inner constitution but by multiple such constitutions. Moreover, even a real essence, if we could discover it, would be relative to an abstract idea (III.vi.6: 442; III.vi.29: 463). For anything to be an "essence" of either the nominal or real sort implies that there is some feature it has necessarily. "But take away the consideration of its being ranked under the name of some abstract *Idea*, and then there is nothing necessary to it, nothing inseparable from it." Thus even a real essence *"relates to a Sort*, and supposes a *Species"* (III.vi.6: 442).

Matters are much more complicated when we come to the question of the ontological status of properties rather than natural kinds. Locke's consistent claims that we are ignorant of the real essences of things presupposes that there is some objective foundation for the resemblances we would detect among things were our senses sufficiently perspicacious to perceive that real constitution.

If we could discover the Figure, Size, Texture, and Motion of the minute Con-stituent parts of any two Bodies, we should know without Trial several of their Operations one upon another, as we do now the Properties of a Square, or Triangle. (IV.iii.25: 556)

This passage reflects Locke's belief that the laws of nature are in principle intelligible, even if they are not intelligible to us now. The picture it suggests is one in which the laws of nature are ultimately the laws of geometry that we could apply a priori if we knew the primary qualities of the corpuscles.[22] This is consistent with Locke's hostility to Aristotelian realism, since there

---

[21] One might think that II.xxiii.3: 296 tells against this interpretation; but there Locke only says that the combinations of simple ideas that go together in experience are "*supposed* to flow from the particular internal Constitution, or unknown Essence of that Substance" (emphasis mine).

[22] See Ayers (1991, vol. 2, ch. 12).

is no suggestion here that objects having similar internal constitutions, and so similar causal powers, form natural kinds. *Which* points of resemblance to take as essential for being of a given kind is up to us, subject to the limits set out above.

How are we to reconcile Locke's denial of real universals with his commitment to properties? Concept nominalism is clearly of no use here, since Locke insists that the resemblances among objects are objective and not a matter for conceptual or linguistic legislation. Many writers argue that Locke holds a kind of resemblance nominalism (henceforth "RN"), according to which the resemblances Locke alludes to are founded on fully particularized properties. The defender of RN must posit such properties on pain of vacuity. For it is always a good question, in virtue of *what* do *a* and *b* resemble one another? If the defender of RN replies simply that it is a brute fact that resemblance obtains, that opens the door for anything to resemble anything else, as D.M. Armstrong points out.[23] Instead, the strongest version of RN casts particularized natures, in Armstrong's phrase, or, as I prefer, particularized properties, to account for resemblance. To say that two things are the same in some respect is not to say that they share in a numerically identical universal, but that they have particular properties related by means of exact resemblance. Like identity, exact resemblance is symmetrical, transitive, and reflexive. It is crucial to see that this view need not be identified with the trope theories of G.F. Stout and D.C. Williams, among others; there is no suggestion here that the properties are ontologically independent of the substances they modify, or that things are "bundles" of properties.[24]

It is not clear to what extent Locke commits himself to this view. We cannot take it for granted that Locke had a fully worked-out view, which needs only to be discovered. He might well have felt himself pulled in different directions. Nevertheless, it does seem true that either the trope theory or the version of resemblance nominalism sketched above must be attributed to Locke if he is to avoid inconsistency. Since his commitment to a substance/attribute ontology is indisputable, it seems clear that the latter view is to be preferred.

Nevertheless, RN faces some serious challenges, foremost among them Russell's regress argument.[25] Russell argues that the appearance of economy RN presents is illusory. RN has seemed attractive primarily because it allows one to avoid positing universals; but Russell argues that this is not in fact the case. Suppose *a* and *b* resemble each other in respect F, that is, they

---

[23] Armstrong (1989, p. 44).   [24] Denkel (1989) makes this point.   [25] Russell (1912, p. 55).

have particularized properties F and F' which resemble each other exactly. Russell now asks, what of this resemblance itself? Is it another particularized property? But then we will need to posit yet another resemblance relation to account for the resemblance between the F and F' and that which holds between F" and F"', where F" and F"' are properties of distinct objects. We are soon involved in a regress; the only way to avoid it is to posit resemblance as a real universal, in which case the apparent economy of RN disappears.[26]

E.J. Lowe suggests that this argument is fatal to Locke's position.[27] But the answer to Russell's regress has in fact come from Armstrong, who in *Universals and Scientific Realism* had himself deployed it against RN. There must be something wrong with Russell's argument, Armstrong argues, because if it were sound it would undermine not just RN, but *every* theory that attempts to account for the apparent phenomena of universals. Even a predicate nominalist will have to posit *applying* as the tie between the predicate and its referents. And the believer in universals must posit *instantiation*.[28] An argument that tells against *all* views on a given topic cannot be held to be decisive. Michael Loux has suggested a different reply to Russell.[29] Russell assumes that the regress is vicious, but it is not obvious that this is so. The infinite hierarchy of resemblances thus generated might be metaphysically uneconomical, but so long as these higher-order resemblances are not invoked by RN to explain the first-order resemblance, the regress is virtuous. RN analyzes the claim that two objects *a* and *b* resemble each other in respect F in terms of the particularized properties, which in turn resemble one another. This analysis might generate, but clearly does not invoke, the higher-order resemblances.

We are now in a position to move forward and ask to what degree Locke's position is a realist one. How far are we constrained by the world in forming our abstract ideas, both of properties and kinds?

It is clear that Lockean real essences, being relative to abstract ideas, are not Aristotelian essences adapted to the corpuscularian or mechanist ontology. They are mind-dependent in a way that prohibits us from pretending that we could ever "carve nature at its joints," no matter how deeply we penetrated into its microscopic structure. Nevertheless, it is quite clear

---

[26] Alan Donagan (1971) suggests an alternative reading, according to which Russell was attempting to show the ineliminability of predicate-terms. But then it is not clear that the argument has any ontological force. See Loux (1978, p. 46) for a discussion of Donagan.

[27] Lowe (1995, p. 163).

[28] Armstrong (1989, p. 54). For a different reply to Russell's regress, see Denkel (1989).

[29] Loux (1978, p. 46).

that at neither the macro- nor the microscopic level are our abstract ideas formed arbitrarily (see III.iii.13: 415; III.vi.28: 455; III.vi.46: 468). Locke often speaks of a "standard" set by nature, according to which we form such ideas. This standard must simply be the co-existence of certain ideas in our experience. Although there is no bar to combining the idea of the head of a tiger with that of the body of a man, such an idea would be useless for practical purposes. This uselessness is then explained in terms of the regular productions of nature. At the corpuscular level we also find objective resemblances founded on particular properties. These properties will be the primary qualities, which would both cause and resemble the ideas we would have of them if our senses were sufficiently acute.

There is a *prima facie* tension between Locke's view of laws of nature and the version of RN attributed to him above. Locke, it seems, wants to claim that objects have the causal powers they do in virtue of their hidden inner constitution. This in turn is explicated in terms of their having certain primary qualities; the interrelations between these qualities explain why in a given circumstance a given effect is produced. These primary qualities are nothing more than a selected subset of the thing's properties. So we can generate an account of laws of nature according to which an exemplification of F brings about, under a certain set of background conditions, an exemplification of G. This claim itself would invoke nomological necessities that Locke might well wish to analyze in terms of the laws of geometry, which, on his view, are synthetic. We thus have the means to ground out the counterfactual claims that seem essential to causation. The problem is that for Locke F and G are fully particular properties. So it seems we can never generate a law of nature that applies in multiple instances. (This concern seems to lie behind Armstrong's challenge to RN.)[30] Unless Locke wishes to hold some version of causal particularism à la G.E.M. Anscombe, and it seems clear he does not, he is stuck.

A natural response on Locke's behalf would be to speak not of individual properties but of resemblance classes founded on those on properties. So an exemplification of F is analyzed not as an exemplification of the universal F but rather the presence of a particularized property that exactly resembles others of its class. The laws of nature will then involve these classes of properties rather than the properties themselves. They will take the form: whenever a particular having a property similar to others in a class defined by resemblance, the presence of a property similar to others in a different class will come about. It will be no objection to say that things do not

---

[30] See Armstrong (1991, p. 489).

have their causal powers in virtue of the resemblance class to which they belong (after all, if there were only one individual object in the universe, it would resemble no others, but still might have causal powers). Locke is free to agree with Armstrong that the properties of things account for their causal powers. It is just that those properties themselves are fully particular. Armstrong's challenge, then, can be met. Although Locke did not himself formulate his position in this way, it is consistent with his other commitments.

One of the virtues of this realist *cum* nominalist position, whether or not I am correct in ascribing it to Locke, is its ability to accommodate our intuition that although nominal essences are human constructions they are not formed arbitrarily. Locke can also claim that an ideal science would appeal to fully particularized properties at the corpuscular level to explain the causal powers of physical objects. Whatever its other defects, these positions serve Locke's purpose well: to provide an alternative to the Aristotelian view without sacrificing the belief that there is in principle an objective foundation for our ascriptions of properties and our belief in causal laws.

At this stage of the present work, we have examined Locke's views of signification, abstraction, and essence. We are now in a position to turn to Locke's application of these views in his anti-Aristotelian project before assessing of his overall position.

CHAPTER 4

Locke contra *the Aristotelians: signification and definition*

With this background in place, we can now see how Locke deploys his linguistic thesis in an argument against the Aristotelians. For Locke's investigations into the nature of language are not gratuitously added on to the rest of the *Essay*. They have a clear polemical purpose: to guard against confusion, both quotidian and philosophical. Locke holds that some of the chief obstacles to the advancement of knowledge stem from an ignorance of the workings of words. In particular, the Aristotelian conception of empirical inquiry as directed at uncovering *de re* definitions stems from a fundamental misconception of the signification of words. Before we can see this, however, we must begin with a sketch of the position under attack.[1]

LOCKE'S OPPONENTS

According to the Aristotelian family of views, definition proceeds by assigning a difference to a genus: thus in the definition of man, animal is the genus, rationality the difference. The *properties* of the thing (such as risibility in humans) flow from its essence; they are not essential, but instead are a result of the essence. Other traits are accidents, which do not flow from the essence. Within accidents, we can distinguish separable ones (such as baldness in humans) from inseparable (such as the blackness of a crow). A definition expresses the essence of a substance;[2] indeed, an essence just *is* the substance, insofar as it is knowable by the intellect.[3] In Aquinas's terminology, "definition" refers to the *definiens*, which is not of subject-predicate form: "definitions . . . do not declare that something is or is not."[4] *Rational*

---

[1] This account is drawn from Thomas Spencer (1628, p. 57ff.), cited in Ayers (1981), and John Sergeant (1984), as well as the works of Aquinas. I am attempting here only to extract what is common to these authors; I go on below to point out their differences.

[2] See, e.g., Aquinas, *De Ente et Essentia* (1993, p. 93).

[3] Aquinas, *Summa Theologica* I, 3, 5, ad.1, in Aquinas (1945, vol. 1, p. 32); see also I, 29, 2. See Etienne Gilson (1956, p. 30).

[4] *Commentary on the Posterior Analytics* I.19 in Aquinas (1970, p. 62).

animal, construed as a real nature, is the definition of human being; similarly, the *definiendum* is not a linguistic entity but a real nature, existing enmattered, outside of the mind.[5] This is not to say, however, that an individual can be defined *qua* individual; for on Aquinas's view, *materia signata,* matter thought of as underlying certain defined dimensions, is the principle of individuation and cannot enter into a definition.[6] To arrive at a definition of Socrates *qua* human being, we must abstract the form, a universal, from the particular entity, Socrates. This means merely that we consider the specific nature apart from its individuating characteristics.[7] A true definition (here, in the sense of a proposition) of "human being" has a predicate that consists of terms signifying the essence of human beings. This essence exists only in individual matter; it is the business of the intellect to know such natures, but not *as* individualized natures. Aquinas offers an account of this process according to which an intelligible species is present in the intellect as a likeness of the thing understood. But it is crucial that we not mistake this intelligible species for the object of thought or definition. It is that by which we understand, not that which is understood.[8]

No Aristotelian is committed to thinking that all our definitions fully capture the real essences of things. Instead, as John Sergeant puts it, "Definitions are the Work of Reflection, and are to *suppose* our Natural Notions, which are the Rough Drafts of Knowledge, Common to us, and to the Vulgar."[9] Nature provides us with notions in experience, for they are the intelligible forms as they exist in the mind abstracted from experience. Thus the business of science is to refine the understanding of the untutored, not supplant it. Although we may include some aspects of the thing's essence in our notion *"confusedly,"*[10] they are present and need only be drawn out by reflection.

---

[5] This, it should be noted, is only the most prominent kind of definition in the Aristotelian tradition. At *Posterior Analytics* II. 8–11, Aristotle introduces another definition of "definition," viz., that which "makes clear why a thing is" (93b37, in Aristotle 1984, vol. 1., p. 155). For example, if we define thunder as the extinguishing of fire in the clouds, we thereby give an account of thunder through its cause. See also *Metaphysics* Z 17, as well as Aquinas's commentary on the relevant chapters of the *Posterior Analytics.* This class of definitions is seldom discussed in the modern period, whether by Aristotelians or their opponents. One important exception to this is Hobbes, who contends that definitions of caused things "must consist of such names as express the cause or manner of their generation" (*De Corpore* 6, in Hobbes 1839–45, vol. 1., p. 81).

[6] *De Ente et Essentia,* in Aquinas (1993, p. 94). Aquinas does, however, argue that matter in general, e.g., flesh and bone in general, can enter into the definition. This "undemarcated" matter itself, it seems, is simply form at a different level, and can be included in a definition: "Socrates' essence differs from human essence [which includes 'flesh and bones in general'] only by being demarcated" (*De Ente et Essentia,* p. 94).

[7] *Summa* I, 85, 1 ad 1, in Aquinas (1945, vol. 1, pp. 813–14).

[8] *Summa* I, 85, 2, in Aquinas (1945, vol. 1, p. 817).   [9] Sergeant (1984, p. 299).

[10] Sergeant (1984, p. 294).

As many writers have noticed, Aristotelianism is hardly homogeneous. Within the camp of those who claim that the categorematic words in a definition signify essences, we can distinguish those, like Aquinas, who distinguish the intentional species from the object of thought, and those, like Locke's contemporaries John Sergeant and Kenelm Digby, who do not. On Aquinas's view, the intentional species is a part of the causal mechanism that allows our thought to be directed to the extra-mental essence and is not itself, in the usual case, an object of thought or definition.[11] What is defined is a thing, and a definition signifies its essence.[12] The distinction between the manner of existence proper to things as they exist in the world and as they exist in the mind is a key part of the Aristotelian tradition. Aquinas, for example, is careful to draw it in his discussion in the *Summa*.[13] Reasonably enough, he claims that this difference in manners of existence means that the intentional species and the enmattered species cannot be numerically identical but only similar.

Seventeenth-century Aristotelians such as Digby and Sergeant offer a different account. Both claim that what is present in the mind is the object of thought. Their novel move is to claim that the mental object is numerically identical with the extra-mental thing, in a sense specified below. Moreover, both misread earlier Scholastics as claiming that the intentional species is what is immediately known. Against this position, Sergeant argues that if what is present in us in the act of intellection were merely the likeness of a thing, we could not be said to understand the thing itself but merely something that imperfectly resembles it. "The Schoolmen . . . invented their *Species Intentionales*; which, if they were not the *Same* with our *Notions*, or the *Things* in our Knowledge, were mere *Resemblances* coined by Fancy, as our Modern *Ideas* generally are."[14] He continues: "If they [intentional species] be *imperfectly like* the Thing, they are no more but mere *Resemblances* of it; then, 'tis already abundantly demonstrated, that the Thing can *never* be known *by them*."[15] Sergeant is referring to an earlier discussion, not of the Schoolmen, but of Locke, where Sergeant writes,

---

[11] See esp. *Summa Theologica* I q. 85 art. 2, in Aquinas (1945, vol. 1, pp. 816–18).

[12] See Aquinas (1970, I.19). Matters are complicated by the fact that Aquinas wants to count only the *definiens* as a definition (1970, I.19.5, II.2.11) and MacDonald (1993, p. 169ff.). The crucial point for my purposes, however, is that the *definiendum* is supposed to be extra-mental and extra-linguistic. For an argument that "it is unacceptable for a definition to be nothing more than a statement explaining the signification of a name," see Aquinas (1970, p. 186).

[13] Aquinas (1945, vol. 1, p. 795): "the intellect, according to its own mode, receives under conditions of immateriality and immobility the species of material and mobile bodies; for the received is in the receiver according to the mode of the receiver."

[14] Sergeant (1984, p. 60).   [15] Sergeant (1984, p. 61).

"That only is Known, which I have *in* my Knowledge, or *in* my Understanding . . . Therefore, if I have *only* the *Idea*, and not the *Thing*, in my
Knowledge or Understanding, I can only know the *Idea*, and *not the Thing*;
and by consequence, I know nothing *without me*, or nothing in Nature."[16]
Kenelm Digby argues in precisely the same way.[17] This argument would
not make sense unless it assumed that what is in the mind is the thing
apprehended or understood, rather than part of the mechanism whereby
the mind is directed to that thing. Sergeant and Digby both insist that
direct realism demands that, in the latter's words, "when we apprehend any
thing, the very thing is in us."[18] On this view, the *definiendum* is a mental
content, the species as it exists immaterially in the mind. Definitions may
be said to be *de re* simply because there is no real distinction between an
idea of a real essence and a real essence: though they have different manners
of existence, they are identical. Sergeant writes, "*A Notion is the very thing
it self existing in my understanding.*"[19] Obviously Sergeant does not mean
that the thing exists materially in the mind. His view is made clear later
in *Solid Philosophy*, where he addresses the objection that the extra-mental
object can be known only by resemblance, since whatever exists in the understanding has immaterial being, and so is not identical with anything
outside the understanding. Sergeant writes,

[Someone might object] that the *Notion* of a Thing (a Stone, for example) has a
Spiritual Manner of Being *in* the *Mind*; whereas the Thing, or Stone, *out of* the
Mind has a *Corporeal* Manner of Being, and therefore 'tis in *some* respect Different
from the Thing; and consequently, not *perfectly* the *Same* with it; and so can only
be barely *like* it, or resemble it. I answer, 'Tis granted that it is *Unlike it*, and so
Different from it, and therefore *not the same* with it, as to the *Manner of Existing*;
but I deny that either its *Existing*, or *Manner of Existing* do enter into the *Notion*
(except in the notion of God, to whom Existence is Essential,) or do *at all* belong
to *it*, or the *Thing* either; but that the *Notion* is the Thing, precisely according to
what is *Common* to it both *in* the Understanding and *out of it*, abstractedly from
both those *Manners of Existing*.[20]

The fact that Sergeant's notions and physical objects have different manners
of existing, since one is immaterial and the other material, does not prevent
them from being identical. Notice how far we are from the Thomistic
conception. Aquinas would argue that the relation of likeness between the

---

[16] Sergeant (1984, p. 30).   [17] Digby (1657, Second Treatise, pp. 3–4).
[18] Digby (1657, Second Treatise, pp. 3–4).
[19] Sergeant (1984, p. 27). Similarly, Kenelm Digby treats the claim that "the very nature of a thing
   apprehended, is truly in the man, who doth apprehend it" as equivalent to the claim that "when we
   apprehend any thing, the very thing is in us" (Digby 1657, Second Treatise, pp. 3–4).
[20] Sergeant (1984, p. 38).

intentional species and the thing represented does not entail that what is *known* is only the likeness, since the intentional species is a causal rather than an epistemic intermediary.

Since Locke rarely names his targets in the *Essay*, it is difficult to know the precise details of the position he takes himself to be attacking. There are passages, however, when he clearly seems to have the Digby/Sergeant position in mind. For example, in Book II, he argues that none of our ideas is itself a real essence (II.xxxi.6: 379); if it were, the properties of anything agreeing with it would "be deducible from it, and their necessary connexion with it . . . known." Aquinas, as we have seen, would not have said that the essence of a thing is the immediate object of thought, at least in the usual case. In what follows, I shall abstract from these differences of doctrine, since there is still a core thesis on which both the seventeenth-century Aristotelians and orthodox Aristotelians agree: words in definitions signify real essences that exist in physical objects. It is this doctrine I have in mind when speaking of "Aristotelianism."

THE STRUCTURE OF LOCKE'S ANTI-ARISTOTELIAN ARGUMENTS

It is useful to divide Locke's arguments against the Aristotelians into two classes: epistemological and metaphysical. The former appeal to our relative benightedness; if our pre-theoretical classificatory scheme mapped on to or even dimly reflected a network of Aristotelian real essences, a number of conditions would have to be met that aren't. The metaphysical arguments, by contrast, suggest that even if our epistemic state were improved to God-like omniscience, there still would be nothing that could play the role of such essences. In its most general formulation, the point Locke wishes to establish by means of both kinds of argument is this: the world, even at the level of its microscopic corpuscular structure, does not force upon us one set of classifications rather than another, since the standards for kind-membership will always invoke an abstract idea. The choice of which objective similarities to count as defining a kind is still a choice, even if it is not purely arbitrary.

The central thesis of this chapter is that there is a third strand of argument that proceeds from the nature of signification. Unlike the other arguments, it is indirect: it seeks to undermine the metaphysical commitments of the Aristotelian by showing how they flow from a fundamental error about the workings of language. Whenever a philosopher attacks an entrenched body of doctrine, it is reasonable to expect an account that not only shows that doctrine to be a mistake but explains why so many intelligent people have made it. These tasks are often tightly woven together. Berkeley, in the introduction to the *Principles*, affords an instance of this strategy: he begins by attempting to sweep away the doctrine of abstract ideas that alone makes belief in necessarily unperceivable objects plausible or perhaps unavoidable. At the same time, he makes a start at showing that materialism is in fact false. On my reading, Locke is engaged in a parallel effort in the case of Aristotelian essences. Central to his case is the linguistic thesis, which he thinks rules out the possibility of *de re* definitions.

It is often acknowledged that the linguistic thesis must have *some* role to play in Locke's anti-Aristotelian argument. After all, Locke's purpose in undertaking the study of language in the first place was, in part, to clear away the rubbish that stands in the way of the mechanical science. But I shall argue that neither of the kinds of argument sketched above accords the linguistic thesis a sufficiently robust role in this project. If we admit only these two families of argument, the link Locke clearly wants to draw between violations of the linguistic thesis and belief in Aristotelian essences will remain obscure.

As much of this is well-traveled ground (ground I have myself partially covered in the previous chapter), I shall offer only a brief account of the epistemological and metaphysical arguments.[21] Let us begin with the latter. The heart of Locke's metaphysical disagreement with the Aristotelians, I suggest, lies in the mechanist ontology.[22] If, as Boyle had claimed, we can in principle account for observable differences among objects in terms of the primary qualities of their corpuscular constitutions, it will make no sense to speak of distinct Aristotelian essences that provide grounds for a division of things into natural kinds. At bottom, all physical things are composed of corpuscles differing only in size and shape. What makes the difference between the Lockean real essence of a horse and that of a donkey is not the presence or absence of a Scholastic form but rather of a certain microphysical structure. As we have seen, Locke is happy to admit the existence of such "real essences" so long as it is clear that they are relative to an idea. Locke

---

[21] The best treatment of these issues is probably Ayers (1981); but see also Bolton (1998a), discussed below.

[22] By contrast, Ayers writes, "Locke's argument hinges on the denial of real universals and on the intuitive ontological principle that everything that exists is particular" (1981, p. 254). I doubt whether this represents Ayers's considered view, even though something like this statement appears in his (1991). It is hard to see how these two points could undermine Aristotelianism, since there clearly are Aristotelian views that endorse both; Súarez, for example, seems to agree that everything is particular and that enmattered universals are perfectly determinate and particular. Moreover, Ayers's own discussions of Locke's argument, on which I draw below, do not explicitly appeal to either point.

does not deny that there are objective resemblances among objects, even at the corpuscular level; what he denies is that these resemblances are sufficient to ground one particular way of sorting those objects as opposed to any other. *Which* resemblances we select to serve as necessary conditions for membership in a given group is entirely up to us. As Ayers puts it, "one mechanical difference is as good a ground for distinction as another – there is no principled difference between them."[23]

It is worth noting that Ayers also discusses what he calls "the argument from language" (see III.viii.1–2: 474–5 and III.x.6: 493),[24] which does not appeal to the linguistic thesis but to the claim that our ability to intelligibly distinguish between a substance and what is supposed to be its essence (as with body and extension, for example) shows that we have not yet pinned down that essence. Descartes, for example, had argued that "Thought and extension can be regarded as constituting the natures of intelligent substance and corporeal substance; they must then be considered as nothing else but thinking substance itself and extended substance itself – that is, as mind and body."[25]

There is only a conceptual distinction between a substance and its essence. But Locke sees a problem here: if in fact the essence of XYZ is PQR, we could never go wrong in replacing occurrences of "XYZ" with "PQR." But when we run this test on proposed essences, we find that we produce gibberish. Thus the claim that extension is the essence of body must be false, since "body" is not replaceable by "extension" *salve veritate* or even *salve congruitate*. This argument tells only against Cartesian essentialism, since orthodox Aristotelianism would deny that a substance is only conceptually distinct from its essence.[26]

Let us now turn to the epistemological arguments. In III.vi.14–19: 448–9, Locke gives a set of conditions that would have to obtain if we were to sort things according to their Aristotelian real essences.[27] First, nature would have to oblige by making only things that clearly fit into one category or another. Locke thinks that the existence of monsters (creatures not clearly

---

[23] Ayers (1997, p. 176).   [24] Ayers (1991, vol. 2, pp. 51–64).

[25] *Principles* §63, in Descartes (1984, vol. 1, p. 215).

[26] See Aquinas, *De Ente et Essentia*, in his (1993). It is not entirely clear where Sergeant stands on this issue, since he seems to think that the sum of a thing's accidents suffices for individuation. Aquinas's resistance to the identification of a substance with its essence stems from the need for *materia signata* to individuate that essence; lacking this motivation, it is not clear whether Sergeant must follow Aquinas here.

[27] Locke lists five conditions, but under the fifth heading he merely adds a lemma to the fourth. The first condition is simply a demand for a "better explication" of the doctrine that "Nature, in the production of Things, always designs them to partake of certain established *Essences*, which are to be the Modes of all Things to be produced."

falling into any of the supposed real species) gives us grounds to doubt either whether nature always "attains" the essence it picks out for a given creature, or, more fundamentally, whether it gives creatures essences at all.[28] For "if History lie not, Women have conceived by Drills; and what real *Species*, by that measure, such a Production will be in Nature, will be a new question" (III.vi.23: 451). Locke reports that he "once saw a Creature, that was the Issue of a Cat and a Rat, and had the plain marks of both about it" (*ibid.*). Although it was common in Locke's age to individuate species according to their capacity to interbreed, these alleged counterexamples are designed to show that this criterion is not sufficient. If we classify things according to their parentage, we ignore the fact that they might well lack many of the traits we took to be associated with the alleged essence. According to Locke, these irregular productions of nature show that we are not confronted with a world that can be "carved at the joints" but rather a continuum of characteristics, where divisions, if there are to be any, must be imposed by us. Is there really a fact of the matter, Locke seems to ask, that can decide whether or not a particularly hideous baby (such as the future Abbot of St. Martin) is "really" a human being?

More fundamentally, Locke argues that if the Aristotelian picture were correct, we ought to have ideas of the real essences, according to which we are allegedly classifying things (III.vi.18: 449). The classificatory difficulties posed by monsters is just one sign of our ignorance of essences. This is a puzzling point since, as we noted above, the claim that we have complete knowledge of essences was no part of Aristotelianism. The Aristotelian, it seems, can happily accept Locke's points, writing off the existence of monsters as perplexing only because of our imperfect knowledge of essences. Leibniz makes this point in the *New Essays*: "It is true that we cannot define a species in terms of something that is unknown to us; but the outer features serve in place of it, though we recognize that they do not suffice for a rigorous definition, and that even nominal definitions in these cases are only conjectural and sometimes . . . merely provisional."[29] These "outer features" are enough to go on, giving us grounds for supposing that there is an essence that explains them. In Aristotelian terms, each essence has a set of properties flowing from it, which might allow us to distinguish things into kinds even in ignorance of that real essence.

Locke, however, blocks this move in the next passage (III.vi.19: 449). If we don't know the essence, how are we supposed to tell which properties

---

[28] This is a somewhat odd way of putting matters, but it follows Locke's own in III.vi.15–6.
[29] Leibniz (1996, p. 311).

flow from it? Any judgment about the necessary connection between a quality and an essence presupposes a knowledge of the latter as well as the former. As Ayers has noted, there might be a tension here in Locke's view.[30] For he sometimes seems happy to allow that the copresence of qualities justifies us in positing a (Lockean) real essence to explain them; the Aristotelian is merely making a parallel move. But when he is more careful, Locke disallows the inference from the copresence of observable features to a single real essence. (See above, chapter three.)

So far, the epistemological points do not seem especially telling against the Aristotelian. One way of putting this point is to say that the Aristotelian conceives of essences primarily as *explanations* for observable phenomena, whereas Locke in these passages seems to construe them as an account of our current classificatory practices. But it is perfectly consistent with Aristotelianism to confess our ignorance of some or perhaps all of these essences.

Perhaps we can reconstruct a robust anti-essentialist argument from these materials, however, if we introduce Locke's considerations about language. This is what Martha Bolton has attempted to do. She sees Locke's opponents as defending a "referentialist" view, according to which our sortal terms can refer to natural kinds even in the absence of an idea of the essence that accounts for the difference among those kinds. It is worth noting that it is not at all clear that the referentialist view was actually held by any of the figures Locke might have had in mind. Indeed, if Ashworth is right, their claim would be that some words signify essences, where "signify" includes aspects of both sense and reference. Let us set this aside and examine Bolton's reconstructed argument.

As Bolton understands III.vi.9: 442ff., Locke invokes two key premises: an abstract idea is what it is immediately perceived to be, and an idea represents exactly those things that agree with it.[31] But if we do not know what a real essence is, then we cannot have an idea of the kind determined by it:

Locke's traditional semantic formula conjoined with this epistemic requirement implies that we *cannot* have a name that signifies things in a kind determined by an *unknown* real essence. It follows at once that the "referential" theory is false. It says we *can* have names for kinds whose boundary-determining essences we do not know.[32]

As this passage suggests, Bolton adopts Ashworth's reading of the thesis, claiming that on Locke's view, we can signify extra-mental things only if

---

[30] Ayers (1991, vol. 2, pp. 79–81).   [31] See Bolton (1998a, p. 220).   [32] Bolton (1998a, p. 219).

we have an idea to which they "agree." Locke and his opponents are said to concur on the nature of language but part ways when it comes to the necessity for a mental object, an idea, to mark off those things that share an essence from all others.

This "idea-theoretic" argument is independent of the question of essentialist metaphysics. For even if such Aristotelian real essences *did exist*, and we knew them, it would still be ideas, and not those essences, that determine kind-membership. The classificatory scheme embodied in our network of abstract ideas would, in such a case, map precisely those distinctions found among species. If successful, then, the idea-theoretic argument shows at most that the extension of an abstract idea is fixed by agreement to that idea, not that its extension cannot include all and only those members of a mind-independent natural kind.[33] This kind of worry, I think, is what has led commentators such as Ayers to hold that the doctrine of abstract ideas is offered, not as an assumed premise in an argument against the essentialists, but rather as an alternative to their theory.[34]

However that may be, we can ask how robust a role the idea-theoretic argument assigns to the linguistic thesis. The crucial premises follow from the very nature of Lockean ideas. Conjoined with *any* of the three understandings of the linguistic thesis (whether my own, Ashworth's, or Kretzmann's), these premises show the "referentialist" view to be false. Indeed, the linguistic thesis, on Bolton's reading, is of a piece with the very body of doctrine Locke takes himself to be attacking.

But at this point we might begin to suspect that our understanding of Book III is impoverished. For Locke clearly thinks that the fact that words signify nothing but ideas *does* play a role in undermining the Aristotelian picture. An interpretation that makes of this thesis a wheel that spins freely cannot be satisfactory. We can begin to assign the thesis its proper role only if we recognize that it is not a bit of Scholastic detritus Locke failed to expunge, but rather part of a tradition deeply at odds with the debased, albeit commonplace, late Scholastic understanding of signification.

THE SECRET REFERENCES

At the start of Book III, Locke discusses two chief abuses to which language is subject: these are the "secret references" that "Men . . . in their Thoughts" give to words (III.ii.4: 406). For "references" we might substitute

---

[33] See Bolton (1998a, p. 225).   [34] See Ayers (1991, vol. 2, p. 66).

"suppositions': Locke's claim is that we are apt tacitly and unthinkingly to suppose that words latch onto things or ideas in the minds of others.[35]

It is seldom noted that there are in fact four secret references, not two. There are four distinct ways one might go wrong: one might refer one's *ideas* to (a) ideas in other men's minds, or (b) the real natures of things; alternatively, one might refer one's *words* to either (a) or (b). Ideas are the focus of II.xxxii.8: 386 (cp. II.xxxi.6: 378), while III.ii.4: 406–7 focuses on words. Most commentators run these four different activities together; Locke himself is not careful to distinguish between them. But there are important differences, and an argument against referring words to real essences, for example, will have to be quite different from an argument against referring *ideas* to real essences.

Let us take up the case of ideas first. It is because we think that our ideas have a "double conformity" with the things we take them to represent *and* with ideas in other men's minds signified by the words of our common language that we secretly refer our ideas to these things, i.e., we suppose that they do in fact so conform. Otherwise, we think we would "both think amiss of Things in themselves, and talk of them unintelligibly to others" (II.xxxii.8: 386). But if ideas are "referred to real Essences as to Archetypes which are unknown" they "cannot be supposed to be any representation of them at all" (II.xxxi.6: 379). To say that I refer my idea to a real essence seems to amount to nothing more than that I *suppose* that my idea is a representation of that essence, and this supposition is always false.

To say that I refer my ideas to those in another's mind is just to say that I suppose that our ideas are tokens of the same type. But this supposition is likely to take place only when we are trying to communicate: our ideas are in danger of falsity (in an attenuated sense, for Locke) when we suppose them "*conformable* to [those] in *other Men's* Minds called by the same common Name; *v.g.*, when the Mind intends, or judges its *Ideas of Justice, Temperance, Religion*, to be the same, with what other Men give those Names to" (II.xxxii.5: 384). Similarly, when we secretly give our words a reference to ideas in the minds of others, we suppose our words to be *signs* of those ideas in them. That is, we suppose that a token of a given word is a reliable indicator of a token of the same idea-type in our interlocutor as it is in us. Thus the secret references of both ideas and words to ideas in others' minds come to the same thing.

---

[35] It should be obvious that Locke does not mean "*Bedeutung*" by "reference" here. See II.xxix.12: 367, where Locke writes that the confusion proper to ideas "still carries with it a secret reference to Names."

The temptation to make these secret references stems both from our desire to communicate and the laziness that sometimes prevents us from bothering to check whether we are in fact communicating at all. Locke writes:

[Men] *suppose their Words to be Marks of the* Ideas *in the Minds also of other Men, with whom they communicate*: For else they should talk in vain, and could not be understood, if the Sounds they applied to one *Idea*, were such, as by the Hearer, were applied to another, which is to speak two Languages. But in this, Men stand not usually to examine, whether the *Idea* they, and those they discourse with have in their Minds, be the same: But think it enough, that they use the Word, as they imagine, in the common Acceptation of that Language; in which case they suppose, that the *Idea*, they make it a Sign of, is precisely the same, to which the Understanding Men of that Country, apply that Name. (III.ii.4: 406)

The situation envisioned here is one in which a speaker supposes that the words he uses as indicative signs of his own ideas are also signs of the same ideas in his hearers. So a speaker might (legitimately) think that his uttered word φ is an indicative sign he gives to his audience of an idea *y* in his mind; but he also might (illegitimately) think φ an indicative sign of the same idea in his speakers. He might run the inference the wrong way. This is more perspicuous if put in the conditional framework provided by Aristotle *et al.*: the right kind of inference occurs when the *hearer* judges, "if *x* speaks φ, then *x* is having an idea of type *z*"; the wrong inference occurs when the *speaker* judges, "if I speak φ, then my hearer is having an idea of type *z*." Again, words are signs only of ideas in the speaker's mind.

The final secret reference to be examined is the most important for our purposes. This consists in supposing our words to be signs of extra-mental things, including real essences.

THE ARGUMENT FROM SIGNIFICATION

Locke's argument for his linguistic thesis (explored above, chapter one) seems so strong that we may doubt whether anyone has ever held that words are signs of things, in Locke's sense. Locke is fully aware that the position he ascribes to his opponent is so ludicrous as to make one suspect he is attacking a strawman. Locke disagrees:

But however preposterous and absurd it be, to make our names stand for *Ideas* we have not, or (which is all one) Essences we know not, it being in effect to make our Words the signs of nothing; yet 'tis evident to any one, whoever so little reflects on the use Men make of their Words, that there is nothing more familiar. (III.x.21: 502)

The fifth abuse of words Locke discusses in III.x consists in "*setting them in the place of Things, which they do or can by no means signify*" (III.x.17: 499). Since "*Men* would not be thought to talk *barely* of their own Imaginations, but of Things as they really are . . . they *often suppose their Words to stand also for the reality of Things*" (III.ii.5: 407). Since our words do not signify real essences, the knowledge they convey is limited to the fact that the speaker is having certain ideas or performing certain operations upon them. Our dissatisfaction with this predicament makes us apt to suppose that the contrary is the case.

On Locke's view, this "secret Supposition" (II.x.18: 500) is part and parcel of our natural tendency to construe categorical statements as making claims about the real essences of things. Locke writes:

[W]hen we put [the names of substances] into Propositions, and affirm or deny any thing about them, we do most commonly tacitly suppose, or intend, they should stand for the real Essence of a certain sort of Substances. For when a Man says *Gold is malleable*, he means and would insinuate more than this, that *what I call Gold is malleable*, (though truly it amounts to no more) but would have this understood, *viz.* that *Gold*; i.e. *what has the real Essence of Gold is malleable*, which amounts to thus much, that *Malleableness depends on, and is inseparable from the real Essence of Gold*. (III.x.17: 499)

In the use of substance words such as "gold," "there is scarce any Body . . . but often supposes each of those names to stand for a thing having the real Essence, on which [its] Properties depend" (III.x.18: 500). The pernicious supposition, then, is that malleableness is a property (in the Aristotelian sense specified above) of gold: while not part of the essence of gold, it flows from and depends upon that essence. This, Locke thinks, is to suppose "gold" the sign of the enmattered real essence of gold, and "malleable," the sign of a property of that essence. Allegedly *de re* definitions involve us in a similar confusion, for the Aristotelian view has it that the *definiendum* is an extra-mental real essence. Locke continues:

Thus when we say, that *Animal rationale* is, and *Animal implume bipes latis unguibus*, is not a good definition of Man; 'tis plain, we suppose the Name *Man* in this case to stand for the real Essence of a Species, and would signifie, that a *rational Animal* better described that real Essence, than *a two-leg'd Animal with broad nails, and without Feathers*. For else, why might not *Plato* as properly make the Word ανθρωπος or *Man* stand for his complex *Idea*, made up of the *Ideas* of a Body, distinguished from others by a certain shape and other outward appearances, as *Aristotle*, make the complex *Idea*, to which he gave the Name ανθρωπος or *Man*, of Body, and the Faculty of reasoning join'd together; unless the name ανθρωπος or *Man*, were supposed to stand for something else, than what it signifies; and to be put in the place of some other thing, than the *Idea* a Man professes he would express by it? (III.x.17: 500)

Locke's point is that there is no motivation for attempting to distinguish good from bad definitions on other than purely pragmatic grounds,[36] or for indulging in disputes about definitions, unless one is laboring under the misapprehension that the word signifies a thing rather than an idea. The only thing necessary is to get our definitions straight, that is, make sure that we are annexing the same idea-type to a given word-type. But this is simply to define a word; it takes us no closer to *de re* definition.

Why is it that words do not signify real essences? It is common enough to declare that definitions are merely *de dicto*. But Locke is not simply stipulating this, as Richard Robinson suggests.[37] Instead, the claim follows from the nature of signification, and the contingent fact that when one says, e.g., "stone," a stone does not thereby materialize. Once one understands what is meant by "sign," the claim should be uncontroversial. In *De Corpore*, Hobbes had already argued in this way that words can only be signs of ideas.[38] Locke makes precisely the same move when he argues that the world *gold* understood as signifying a real essence "comes to have no signification at all": "by this tacit reference to the real Essence of that Species of Bodies, the Word *Gold* . . . comes to have no signification at all, being put for somewhat, whereof we have no *Idea* at all, and so can signify nothing at all, when the Body itself is away. (III.x.19: 501; discussed above, chapter one). If a sign serves as an evidence for what it signifies in virtue of being a signal or indicator of its significate, it would be absurd to say that a word can signify the real essence of gold. If we had an idea of the essence, we could, of course, signify it; in the absence of the physical stuff, "gold" would signify our idea of its real essence. But as matters stand, if "gold" were a sign for the physical stuff, or for its real essence, it could be a sign only when the speaker is in the presence of gold. "When the body itself is away," the word no longer indicates or signals anything. If a sign is an indication, one can, of course, use a word to signify an extra-mental thing such as gold: one simply utters the word when and only when one is in the presence of gold. One might, in this way, become a gold-indicator. But although words *can* signify extra-mental things in this way, this is not the purpose for which they were designed. This option would hardly be

[36] See III.iv.6: 422.   [37] Robinson (1950, p. 9ff.).
[38] *De Corpore* I.ii.5 in Hobbes (1839–45, vol. 1, p. 17), quoted above.

attractive to Locke's Aristotelian opponents, and the linguistic thesis is not compromised by his admitting the possibility of signifying things in this way. If anything, it makes the structure of Locke's argument for the thesis more perspicuous: words signify ideas precisely because of the special tasks for which we employ them (III.ii; see II.xi.8–9).

The linguistic thesis is not an a priori truth; it flows instead from the sort of work we expect words to do and the sort of things with which they can be so correlated as to fund inferences. In order to use language, one must "be *able to use these* [articulate] *Sounds, as Signs of internal Conceptions*; and to make them stand as marks for the *Ideas* within his own Mind, whereby they might be made known to others . . ." (III.i.2: 402). This means that one cannot offer a *de re* definition simply because there is no way for the real essence to stand in the place of the *definiendum*: what one defines is a word, not a thing. This kind of definition consists merely in setting out the idea with which the word is customarily linked.[39]

Let us be clear about the logical structure of the argument from signification. It is designed to function independently of the more familiar planks of Locke's anti-essentialist position, such as the theory of abstract ideas and the mechanist ontology. The linguistic thesis itself is a consequence of the nature of signs, together with obvious (but contingent) facts about the sorts of things one can profitably use words to signify. According to Locke, considerations about the nature and purpose of language suffice to undermine the project of attaining *de re* definitions. Given that words are conventional signs or indications, they can signify neither objects in a public environment nor their enmattered real essences.

If successful, the argument from signification would undermine crucial parts of Scholastic doctrine, particularly those pertaining to science. For Aristotelian science is essentially classificatory: it proceeds via demonstration on the basis of definitions. If these definitions turn out to be merely nominal in Locke's sense, so does all that is built upon them. What is more, categorical predications other than definitions were construed by the Aristotelian as being true or false in virtue of the relation between an essence and the properties flowing from it; now their truth or falsity depends instead on the contents of a speaker's mind.

The most obvious charge against Locke's argument is simply that no one has ever held the position he attacks. It would indeed be absurd to think that words are indicators of the sorts of physical objects of which

---

[39] "For Definition being nothing but making another understand by Words, what *Idea*, the term defined stands for . . ." (III.x.iii: 413).

we desire *de re* definitions. The Aristotelian might protest that Locke is just equivocating on "signify," substituting his use of the word for theirs. Thus the first line of resistance Locke's argument will meet is a challenge to the claim about language on which it is based, viz., that words are signs in the sense I have been suggesting. In order to meet this challenge, Locke will advert to the purpose of words: their use is to inform others of our own conceptions and mental acts performed on those conceptions, such as combination and separation (III.i.2: 402; see also II.xi.19: 159 and III.ii.1: 404–5). According to Locke, this entails that words are signs in Hobbes's sense, and the argument examined above is then deployed to show that words can be signs in this sense only of mental acts and contents. To the charge of equivocation, then, Locke will reply that his opponent has been mistaken all along about the nature of language; once the Aristotelian properly understands this nature, he will see how absurd his view really is.

One might also object that Locke's point has no teeth, since he seemingly allows a notion of reference to be constructed out of signification (see above, chapter one). If we can truly say that "man" refers to man, "rational," to a certain quality, and "animals" to animals, why can we not generate a *de re* definition of man?[40] But recall that notions of reference so constructed must be treated as a shorthand for a cumbersome analysis: to say that "animals" refers to animals is just to say that someone speaking that word in certain contexts is liable to have an idea of the class or sort *animals* in his head. And this sortal idea is a purely nominal essence. So although Locke is happy to allow that words in an attenuated sense "refer to" things, once a proper analysis is provided, we can see that this does not entail that *de re* definitions are possible. The *definiendum* and *definiens* are still ideas.

What about those other notions Locke sometimes uses, such as "mark," "denote," and "design?" Clearly he sometimes speaks of words latching onto things by means of these relations. We now have indirect support for my claim above (chapter one) that Locke wishes to allow these relations only so long as they receive the proper analysis, as sketched above. It seems true that if Locke *did* think that words signify ideas but unproblematically and unanalyzably refer to things, his disagreement with the Aristotelian would be a purely verbal one. The linguistic thesis would have no anti-essentialist implications. But this is so plainly false that I do not see how we can take this suggestion seriously. In addition, I have argued against this position above at some length.

---

[40] I am grateful to Harold Langsam for making this objection to me.

We can see the instability of Locke's terminology in this passage from earlier in the *Essay*:

The next thing to be considered is, by which of those Essences it is, that *Substances are determined into* Sorts, or *Species*; and that 'tis evident, is *by the nominal Essence*. For 'tis that alone, that the name, which is the mark of the Sort, signifies. 'Tis impossible, therefore, that any thing should determine the Sorts of Things, which we rank under general Names, but that *Idea*, which that Name is design'd as a mark for. (III.vi.:7: 443)

This brief passage occurs in the heart of the epistemological argument of III.vi, and anticipates the argument from signification of III.x. Here Locke uses "mark" to refer both to a relation between words and ideas and between words and things. This imprecision is liable to obscure the main point, which I think is clear enough: since only ideas (nominal essences) can be signified by words, it is absurd to suppose that a real essence fixes the sorts of things we use our words to "refer" to (in the attenuated sense specified above). Here, Locke explicitly uses the linguistic thesis to ground the claim that nominal, and not real, essences fix the boundaries of sorts. This indicates the complexity of Locke's strategy. We should be wary of taking any one of his arguments as fundamental, since he connects them to form a sophisticated web of anti-Aristotelian considerations. If my interpretation is correct, Locke's argument from signification must take its place in this web alongside the epistemological and metaphysical arguments.

This argument attempts to move from a view about the nature of language to the conclusion that the project of attaining *de re* definitions is incoherent. Now, this is surely not the first time that a philosopher has thought considerations about the nature of language relevant to epistemological and metaphysical concerns. Locke takes his place in the Baconian tradition of heaping scorn upon the "learned Gibberish" of the Schoolmen. But he does more than this: he presents a developed theory of the nature of language he thinks capable of cutting Aristotelian nonsense off at the root and showing up pretensions to *de re* definition.

CHAPTER 5

Beyond the bounds of sense?

Locke's deployment of his linguistic thesis against the Aristotelians raises the specter of self-refutation. For all we have said so far, it is unclear how Locke can argue that the Aristotelians talk nonsense because they use categoremata without corresponding ideas while helping himself to discussions of God, real essence, and substance. In all three cases, Locke denies that experience provides us with ideas of these things. In order to make room for significant speech about that which lies beyond the bounds of experience, Locke must relax the linguistic thesis; but if he is not to vitiate his arguments against the Aristotelians, he must be wary of giving too much ground. I shall argue that Locke's considered view accomplishes precisely this. The goals of the present chapter are twofold: to show that Locke escapes self-refutation and, perhaps more importantly, to deepen and in some respects revise our understanding of the linguistic thesis.

NONSENSE

As we have seen, Locke's thesis that words signify ideas and acts in the mind of the person speaking them imposes a limit on the senseful use of language. The argument we have been examining is an instance of what Irving Thalberg has called the "argument from nonsense,"[1] common throughout modern and later empiricism. Such an argument tries to show that a given claim is not false but nonsensical. "Nonsense" has several different senses: we sometimes apply it to obviously false statements or to the gibberings of infants. Philosophically interesting nonsense, however, uses words that have been given other uses in the language to make claims that are not merely false but literally without sense. We can distinguish two kinds of argument from nonsense: verificationist and ideational. Locke, Berkeley, and Hume all deploy the latter, requiring that categoremata, with

---

[1] See Thalberg (1981).

some exceptions, be correlated with mental contents that can in turn be traced back to an initial experience, or constructed out of contents that can be thus traced. With the advent of Frege's context principle, philosophers came to see the entire sentence rather than the word as the smallest unit of meaning. Empiricists such as Ayer accordingly rejected ideational arguments from nonsense, since these depend on an isomorphic relation between categoremata and ideas, and thus on the supposition that words can have meaning outside the context of a sentence. While the traditional argument from nonsense was genetic, since it asked for the experiential credentials of any allegedly significant categorematic word, verificationist arguments are forward-looking. The question becomes, not whether a speaker has the experiential credentials to use a given word in a given way, but whether the claim the speaker is making is one for which he can in principle describe experiences that would tell either for or against that claim.

Despite the clear difference between these two kinds of argument, both can be found in early modern empiricism. Although the verificationist form of the argument from nonsense is rarely explicit in earlier thinkers, it is implicit in passages such as the following from Berkeley's *Principles*: "[I]f there were external bodies, it is impossible we should ever come to know it; and if there were not, we might have the very same reasons to think there were that we have now" (*P* 20). The hypothesis that there are external objects is one that experience itself could never decide. Berkeley does not draw the conclusion a positivist would, namely, that the hypothesis is therefore meaningless. Berkeley uses very different grounds to argue that the materialist position is unintelligible; this is his famous "master argument" (see *P* 22–4). Despite this, it is not fanciful of Ayer to see in Berkeley a precursor to his own brand of empiricism,[2] for Berkeley clearly thinks that a central problem with the materialist[3] *cum* representationalist picture is that no experience can ever be relevant to ascertaining its truth or falsity. This is closely connected with another of Berkeley's points, namely that an external world is explanatorily otiose: it does no work in accounting for our experiences that cannot be done with a more modest ontology, one that includes only God and finite minds.

To this extent the verificationist argument from nonsense was prefigured in the modern period. But alongside this kind of argument, we find in both Berkeley and Hume a more straightforward demand that for any senseful

---

[2] Ayer (1946, p. 31).
[3] I am using "materialism" (as Berkeley did) to refer to the position that a material world exists.

categorematic word, one be able to advert to an item of experience from which the idea that the word signifies was derived.[4] Someone offering the verificationist argument need not be concerned with how the individual words of a given claim get their meaning; the verificationist takes as his target the proposition as a whole. By contrast, the ideational argument from nonsense deals with the particular categorematic words making up such a claim. What is at issue there is not whether the claim itself can be verified, but whether experience provides the ideas that make the categoremata of the claim meaningful.

That Locke is the most immediate source for this earlier form of the argument from nonsense will already be apparent. His linguistic thesis, in a sense we have yet to specify, identifies the bounds of sense with the bounds of experience. The purpose of this chapter is to clarify and evaluate Locke's position in light of his own metaphysical commitments: can Locke affirm the linguistic thesis while helping himself to the very metaphysical notions later empiricists such as Berkeley, Hume, and Ayer were to reject as nonsensical?

Let us begin by examining the varieties of nonsense Locke thinks we are apt to commit. The first of six "abuses of words" Locke discusses in III.x[5] is the "most palpable": using words either with no ideas at all or without a clear and distinct idea. When this happens, debates inevitably arise that are pointless not only because the parties involved are talking past each other but because they are using words without (clear and distinct) ideas, making their disagreement merely verbal. In philosophy, this most often happens when metaphysicians coin new words "without much troubling their Heads to examine, what are the precise *Ideas* they stand for" (III.x.2: 491). The "great Mint-Masters" of such terms, the Schoolmen, were apt to paper over genuine difficulties by introducing new words whenever it suited them, without specifying the ideas they were to signify.

Nonsense also results when we attempt to give words a signification they cannot have. The Aristotelian obsession with definitions springs from this abuse of words, as we saw in the previous chapter. In such cases, the Aristotelians have not coined new words but simply made a mistake about the workings of language. Existing words that in ordinary discourse serve perfectly well to indicate ideas in the mind of the speaker are taken to

---

[4] I am neglecting here Berkeley's doctrine of notions, according to which words referring to minds can be significant even if they are not associated with any idea. I discuss this doctrine in more detail in the next chapter. I am also abstracting from the issue of the precise meaning of signification in these later figures. I address this with regard to Berkeley in the next chapter as well.

[5] We need not be detained by the other abuses of words Locke discusses in III.x.

signify extra-mental objects and their real essences instead. As a result, we end up with familiar words that taken in their proper signification are unobjectionable but when put to the use the Aristotelian requires signify nothing at all. This confusion explains why the Aristotelians would wish to place philosophical weight on definitions, weight they cannot bear. From Locke's point of view, the whole metaphysical system of forms and essences rests on this confusion about the nature of language. When one tries to give words a signification they cannot have, one produces not genuine speech (or writing) but mere sounds (or squiggles on a page). The words are divorced from their fundamental role as tools for revealing our thoughts to one another, and so become nonsense. This argument, then, is just a special case of the ideational argument.

Although arguments from nonsense can be quite powerful, they also have a tendency to turn on the philosopher who uses them. Notoriously, the principle of verification cannot itself be verified, and so the position seems self-refuting.[6] Locke's ideational argument is not vulnerable to the same charge. But if Locke is going to set limits to senseful discourse, he must be careful of violating those very limits in stating his own position. The ideational argument from nonsense threatens not only Scholastic metaphysics but Locke's metaphysics as well. We shall look at three concepts that are central to Locke's view, and for which we do not seem to have the requisite ideas.

SEMIOTIC EMPIRICISM

We must begin with a more careful statement of what we might call Locke's "semiotic empiricism," revising a phrase of Bennett's.[7] As a first approximation, consider:

(1) Every meaningful categorematic word, when used by S, must signify an idea in the mind of S; that idea must come from either sensation or reflection.

So stated, the doctrine is unclear. What sense of "comes from experience" is intended? Is it necessary that the idea be *given* in experience, or merely that experience provide the materials from which the idea can be

---

[6] This is to ignore, of course, other means of retaining the verification principle, such as van Fraassen's suggestion that it embodies a "stance" rather than a claim about meaningfulness.

[7] According to Bennett, Locke's "semantic empiricism" is the claim that "no classificatory word makes sense to us unless either (a) we have sensorily encountered things to which it applies, or (b) we can define it in terms of words which satisfy (a)" (1971, p. 26). That this is not Locke's position will become apparent.

constructed? We might call these views narrow and wide semiotic empiricism, respectively. At some points Locke seems committed to the narrow
view, as when he writes, "the simple *Ideas* we receive from Sensation and
Reflection, are the Boundaries of our Thoughts; beyond which, the Mind,
whatever efforts it would make, is not able to advance one jot" (II.xxiii.29:
312; see II.xxxii.25: 393). At other times, however, Locke is well aware of
his need to allow for ideas that have been built on the simple ideas. Right
at the start of Book II, for example, we are told that although there is no
idea that has not been "imprinted" through sensation or reflection, these
ideas can be "with infinite variety compounded and enlarged by the Understanding" (II.i.5: 106). Evidently Locke thought it unnecessary to mention
abstraction, as this would not, strictly speaking, produce new ideas out of
old but only separate some features from others, or some simple ideas out
of a single complex one (see above). Locke's semiotic empiricism is thus
better captured by:
(2) Every meaningful categorematic word, when used by S, must signify
an idea in the mind of S; that idea must either be given immediately in
sensation or reflection or constructed out of ideas that have been so given.

This chapter has the twofold purpose of tracing out the consequences of
(2) for Locke's overall position and revising our conception of his semiotic
empiricism as we go. For although (2) seems to capture Locke's intent, it
is not clear that it allows Locke to say that "God," "substance," and "real
essence" are significant. I shall argue that these ideas ineliminably involve
mental acts and that Locke must therefore revise (2) to allow for words
that are significant in virtue of signifying *both* mental objects and acts. We
have already seen that Locke is happy to allow that some words, namely,
syncategoremata, signify mental acts; my claim now is that Locke must also
allow that some categoremata signify acts as well as objects. The tension in
Locke's view, I shall argue, stems from his wish to reconcile his use of the
semiotic thesis as a tool for eliminating nonsense and his recognition that
there are some things of which we have no adequate idea.

It is useful to see Locke's project in light of the debate between Hobbes
and the Port-Royalians. Hobbes had objected to Descartes that we do
not in fact have the idea of God on which Descartes based his Third
Meditation proof of God's existence. For Hobbes, an idea is simply an
image. As Descartes points out, he and Hobbes simply disagree over the
nature of ideas. Descartes acknowledges that there can be no Hobbesian
idea (image) of God. By contrast, the Cartesian idea of God is a paradigm
case of an idea that could *not* have come from experience and so could not be
an image. What is relevant for our inquiry is that although Hobbes denies

that we have an idea of God he nevertheless thinks the term meaningful. Hobbes's solution seems to be that "God" becomes meaningful not by being associated with an idea, but in virtue of abbreviating a definite description. Hobbes writes,

Just as a person born blind who has often been brought close to a fire, and feeling himself growing warm, recognizes that there is something that is warming him, and, on hearing that this is called "fire," concludes that fire exists, even though he does not know what shape or color it has, and has absolutely no idea or image of fire appearing in his mind; just so, a man who knows that there ought to be some cause of his images or ideas, and some other cause prior to this cause, and so on, is led finally to an end of this series, namely to the supposition of some eternal cause which, since it never began to be, cannot have a cause prior to itself, and necessarily concludes that something eternal exists. Nevertheless, he has no idea that he could call the idea of this eternal something . . .[8]

Hobbes must deny that every significant categorematic word is associated with an idea. For he wishes to say that there are words that are significant even though they cannot be linked with an idea; this class includes not only "God" but "substance." Hobbes writes, "we do not have an idea of substance. For substance . . . is something that is established solely by reasoning; it is not something that is conceived, or presents any idea to us."[9] We are entitled to go on talking of substance only because that word is linked with a definite description, just as "God" means "that first, eternal cause."[10] Hobbes distinguishes between what is known by experience and what is known by rational inference. Experience provides us with images of things, whereas rational inference gives us only the assurance that there *is* something that fits a certain description. It is vital for Hobbes that the limits of language extend more widely than the limits of our ideas.

The Port-Royalian rejoinder comes in *La Grammaire*: "Had we no idea of God, then in pronouncing the word 'God,' we would conceive only the letters 'g,' 'o,' and 'd.' "[11] On their view, it would be a contradiction to maintain that one does not associate an idea with a given word but nevertheless understands what that word means.[12]

---

[8] Third Objections in Descartes (1984, vol. 2, p. 127).   [9] Descartes (1984, vol. 2, p. 130).

[10] Hobbes's position on the use of "God" is complicated by his suggestion in *Leviathan* that the word is used not so that we may conceive of God but "that we may honour him" (Hobbes 1839–45, vol. 3, p. 11). This suggests an emotive or prescriptive account. But Hobbes does not develop this suggestion.

[11] Arnauld and Nicole (1966, p. 67). Locke's argument at III.vi.49: 470 (examined above, chapter one) is strikingly similar.

[12] Arnauld and Nicole (1970, p. 67): "Car il y auroit de la contradiction entre dire que je sais ce que je dis en pronançant un mot, & que neanmoins je ne conçois rien en le prononançant que le son même du mot."

I shall argue that Locke's central project in accounting for our ability to speak of things that lie beyond the bounds of experience is to reconcile these two accounts. For Locke clearly wants to maintain, with Arnauld and Nicole,[13] that each categorematic word must be associated with an idea. Failure to do so is responsible for much confusion (see III.x.2: 490–1). But at the same time, Locke is skeptical of claims to have informative or substantive conceptions of God, real essence, and substance. Thus he finds congenial the line taken by Hobbes in the third *Objections*, viz., that we can only be said to think of these things by means of a definite description. Yet Locke does not want to deny that we have ideas of them, for this would be to give up a favorite tool of abuse.

What way out, then, is open to Locke? It is somewhat different in each of the three cases we shall examine. There is a common thread, however: in each case Locke denies that there is a single mental object corresponding to the word in question and claims instead that the word signifies a string of mental objects and acts. This leads Locke to claim that the ideas in question are obscure or confused, despite the fact that they succeed in representing real things or qualities. Let us begin with Locke's attempt to answer Descartes's challenge: how can an idea of God be generated on the basis of experience?

GOD

Having rejected Descartes's innatist and intellectualist conception of ideas, Locke finds himself obliged to explain how we can arrive at an idea of God using only the materials furnished by experience. These materials are simple ideas of reflection, such as existence, duration, knowledge, power, pleasure, and happiness (II.xxiii.33: 314; note that pleasure and happiness are absent from the corresponding list in II.xvii.1).[14] We take these simple ideas and then "enlarge" them with our idea of infinity. This does not yield an idea of God's essence, but only "the most suitable" idea of God we can frame. However inadequate this idea might be, it must nevertheless truly represent God; otherwise it would cease to be an idea *of* God.

This method differs significantly from that of the Scholastic empiricists, especially Aquinas and Cajetan. For these figures, theological discourse must make use of analogy. Extending Aquinas's account, Cajetan argues that an analogy of proportionality allows us to speak of God's attributes. This kind

---

[13] See *La Grammaire* I.i (1966, p. 67).
[14] Power is a special case here, since Locke suggests elsewhere that sensation also affords us an idea of power. He claims only that it is in reflection that we attain the *clearest* idea we can have of it.

of analogy is best made clear by an example: "to see by corporeal vision and by intellectual vision are indicated by the term *to see*, because just as *to understand* presents something to the mind, so *to see* presents something to the corporeal body."[15] We can attain a grasp of God's attributes by treating them as analogous to human attributes in this way: thus, we might say that God's wisdom is to God as man's wisdom is to man. This doesn't tell us much about the nature of God's wisdom but at least allows us to conceive of the relation between God and his wisdom. As Cajetan points out, analogy of proportionality involves equivocation: "wisdom," in our example, is not used in the same sense throughout. Indeed, Cajetan rules out the analogy of inequality (where two things are said to "unequally participate" in a single nature, e.g., "body" applied to plants and the celestial bodies) precisely because it uses its terms univocally. It is not immediately clear why Locke eschews the analogy of proportionality as a means of conceiving of God, although his consistent hostility to metaphorical and non-univocal uses of language might lie at the bottom of it (see, e.g., III.xi.26: 523; IV.viii.11: 616; and IV.xvii.13: 683).[16] This is just as well, since the analogy of proportionality is uninformative. If the above example were to provide us with an understanding of the relation between God and his wisdom, we would have to have antecedent knowledge of at least one of those two relata. The "God" side of the equation, as it were, is blank.

By contrast, Locke offers two slightly different accounts of how we "enlarge" our ideas, at II.xvii and II.xxiii.32–3, respectively. I shall argue that one tension in his account concerns *which* ideas we can be said to "enlarge" with our idea of infinity, a point on which Locke seems to have vacillated. Another tension, more interesting for our purposes, concerns the negative idea of infinity and whether it can be said to be a single mental object rather than a complex of mental object and act. Let us begin by examining Locke's two accounts of the formation of an idea of God.

Locke argues at length in II.xvii that we do not have a positive idea of infinity. An idea of infinity would be positive if it represented the entire infinite class under consideration. Locke's argument that we cannot conceive such an idea depends on an appeal not to our cognitive limitations but to the nature of infinity itself: since an infinite set is one in which it is always possible to proceed to the next item in the series, no single idea could ever be adequate to it. For constructing a positive idea, of no matter how large a class, necessarily imposes a limit on that class, and so is inconsistent with

---

[15] Cajetan (1953, p. 25). For a fuller treatment of Cajetan and Aquinas, see Ott (1997).
[16] See Ott (1997) for further discussion.

infinity (see II.xvii.8: 214). The only idea of infinity we have comes from the consciousness of the power of our own minds to go on with a given series without ever coming to the end of it. Locke says that "the Power, we observe in our selves, of repeating without end our own *Ideas*" (II.xvii.6: 212) gives us our idea of infinity. This seems strange, since we have no such power (as a practical matter, there is a limit to our ability to "repeat" our own ideas). Locke's point seems to be instead that the negative idea of infinity arises from our awareness of the possibility *in principle* of continuing to repeat our ideas. We know that however vast the intentional object of our idea of space, we can always in principle add the idea of another foot or mile. Our "growing and fugitive" (II.xvii.12: 216) idea of infinity does not provide us with a conception of the whole infinite series as such. Nevertheless, we must begin with a positive idea. Locke writes,

The *Idea* of Infinite, has, I confess, something of positive in all those things we apply to it. When we would think of infinite Space or Duration, we at first step usually make some very large *Idea*, as, perhaps, of Millions of Ages, or Miles . . . All that we thus amass together in our Thoughts, is positive, and the assemblage of a great number of positive *Ideas* of Space or Duration. But what still remains beyond this, we have no more a positive distinct notion of, than a Mariner has of the depth of the Sea, where having let down a large portion of his Sounding-line, he reaches no bottom: Whereby he knows the depth to be so many fathoms, and more; but how much that more is, he hath no distinct notion at all. (II.xvii.15: 217–18)

Although there is a positive element in our idea of infinity, namely, an idea of a determinate but very large space or duration, we would not have an idea *of* infinity unless we also conceived that there is something beyond this positive element. In the case of God, we can say that God has all the knowledge we humans do, but we must add that his knowledge extends infinitely.

Here we run into a difficulty. For Locke accepts what we might call the "mereological principle": "finite" and "infinite" are "looked upon by the Mind, as the *Modes of Quantity*, and . . . attributed primarily in their first designation only to those things which have parts" (II.xvii.1: 209). This is because the idea of infinity is really nothing but the infinity of number applied to determinate parts (II.xvii.10: 215). "Those *Ideas* that consist not of Parts, cannot be augmented to what proportion Men please, or be stretched beyond what they have received by their senses" (II.xvii.6: 213). Whiteness, for example, cannot be imagined infinite, for there are no discrete parts of this simple quality that one can imagine being repeated forever. If one imagines a foot of a white surface, one can indeed apply the idea of infinity, but only in respect of the idea of the determinate distance, not that of the whiteness.

In II.xvii, Locke sees that the mereological principle will make trouble for his account of how we generate an idea of God. In the case of God's duration and ubiquity, there is no problem, since we have determinate elements that we repeat in our minds with the awareness that such repetition could go on for ever. But can the same be said for God's other qualities, such as power, wisdom, and goodness? Here Locke gives two different answers. In II.xvii.1: 210, Locke claims that we "primarily" speak of God as infinite in time and space, and only "figuratively" speak of his being infinitely powerful, wise, and good. Here, as in III.i.5: 403, a word's "primary" signification or "first designation" is simply its literal use.[17] Moreover, Locke does not include pleasure and happiness as traits we might ascribe to God, although he does do so in II.xxiii.

Locke, however, does not rest content with this account for long. As I have suggested, he might well have been uneasy with relying on metaphor to provide an idea of God. His proposed solution in II.xxiii.32–3 is not to deny the mereological principle, but to argue that some qualities other than extension in space and time also admit of parts. In the case of knowledge, for example, he now claims that he can frame an idea of knowing twice as much as he knows now, simply by doubling the number of things he now knows. This assumes that there is in fact a determinate number of propositions a person knows at any given time, which is doubtful at best. Locke's account of knowledge as the perception of agreement or disagreement between ideas allows him to assume that the mental propositions known are those that can be called into consciousness and thus that knowledge admits of quantity.

By doubling his idea of knowledge, Locke thinks he can extend it to represent knowledge of "all things existing, or possible" (II.xxxii.34: 315). This would bring the idea of infinite knowledge into line with the mereological principle. But Locke goes on to violate this principle by claiming to extend his idea of knowledge by imagining knowing things more perfectly. It is hard to see how the *perfection* of knowledge could be given parts beyond simply numbering the propositions known. Locke goes on to say that the same process can be carried out with power, wisdom, and goodness. But this again seems problematic. Perhaps Locke's thought is that we can look upon *acts* involving these qualities as "units"

---

[17] Contrast the use made of "primary" signification by Ashworth and Kretzmann, discussed above, chapter one.

of those qualities and so generate a negative idea of their infinity that still accommodates the mereological principle. It would be important for Locke to stipulate that the acts in question include not just the actual but the possible exercises of God's attributes, since only the latter would be infinite.

We have seen that Locke is less than consistent in his account of how we generate the idea of God. I now propose to turn to the core of that conception and ask whether it is consonant with Locke's semiotic empiricism as represented by (2) above.

The negative idea of infinity contains an irreducibly propositional element: we must be conscious *of the fact that* however often we repeat one of our ideas, we will never have attained an idea that is adequate to its object in the sense of fully representing every member of the series. Locke's denial of a positive idea of infinity is a denial of the claim that there is a single mental content lying behind the word "infinity." Instead, we have a hodgepodge of mental acts and objects: we have the positive component of the idea (the idea of a determinate number of units or parts of a given thing), but there is also the awareness of the fact that this positive component does not exhaust the infinite thing, quality, or series. This absence of a single object is, I believe, the source of Locke's conviction that the idea of infinity is confused (II.xvii.15: 218), obscure, and "fugitive." When we turn to real essence and substance, we shall see further instances of this same predicament.

Of course, none of this means that on Locke's view the idea of God or its components fails to pick out the proper object. If that were Locke's claim, there would be no point in offering proofs of God's existence, since "God" would signify an idea that does not represent God, and might represent, say, Schmod instead.[18] It simply means that although we can posit the existence of a being with these infinite attributes, we must be careful not to claim that we have an idea that represents God in all his infinitude.

REAL ESSENCE

Locke faces a parallel difficulty in the case of real essences. For Locke consistently says that we have no ideas of real essences, and yet somehow "real essence" is significant. In the following passage, he shows that he is fully aware that his semiotic thesis is in danger of rendering much of the *Essay* nonsensical:

[18] See Ott (1999).

I must beg pardon of my Reader, for having dwelt so long upon this Subject, and perhaps, with some Obscurity. But I desire, it may be considered, how *difficult* it is, *to lead another by Words into the Thoughts of Things, stripp'd of those specifical differences* we give them: Which Things, if I name not, I say nothing; and if I do name them, I thereby rank them into some sort, or other, and suggest to the Mind the usual abstract *Idea* of that *Species*; and so cross my purpose. For to talk of a *Man*, and to lay by, at the same time, the ordinary signification of the Name Man, which is our complex *Idea*, usually annexed to it; and bid the Reader consider *Man*, as he is in himself, and as he is really distinguished from others, *in his internal Constitution, or real Essence, that is, by something, he knows not what, looks like trifling: and yet thus one must do, who would speak of the supposed real Essences* and Species *of Things, as thought to be made by Nature; if it be but only to make it understood, that there is no such thing signified by the general Names, which Substances are called by.* (III.vi.43: 465–6; last emphasis mine)

It is suggestive that Locke uses the same formula ('something he knows not what') for real essence that he usually associates with substance. In both cases, Locke needs some way of talking about something that is beyond experience unless he is to be in the paradoxical position of using a word in order to deny that there is an idea corresponding to it. This would not amount to a powerful anti-Scholastic argument, but rather to a confession that the words he has just set down are themselves nonsense. Locke's position must have the resources to talk about what is beyond experience if the division between sense and nonsense is not to collapse in on itself.

But how is Locke entitled to this, given that he holds that each categorematic word must stand for an idea? The internal constitution is not wholly mysterious, since, as Locke says, "I have an *Idea* of Figure, Size, and Situation of solid Parts in general, though I have none of the particular Figure, Size, or putting together of Parts, whereby the Qualities [of the object] are produced" (II.xxxi.6: 380). If we did not have an idea of what kind of the thing the real essence was, Lockean real essences would be in no way more intelligible or defensible than Aristotelian forms. The point remains that "real essence" cannot designate a single idea, or even a finite number of ideas, since a real essence is not just an idea of figure, size, and position "in general," but rather of that particular arrangement, whatever it is, on which the qualities of an object depend.

But if this is right, Locke must allow that a word can make sense to us because it signifies ideas *and* acts of the mind at once. It seems to me that Locke is thinking that "real essence" signifies the ideas and acts that make significant a definite description such as "the real internal constitution of a thing on which its discoverable properties depend." Such phrases make ineliminable use of words Locke does not allow to be associated with ideas, such as "the," "such," and so on. It does seem that *any* definite description, although not itself a complete proposition, must involve syncategoremata. Thus, as in the case of "God," we must refine (2) to allow that a word might have its meaning, not by being correlated with a single idea (be it simple or complex), but rather with several ideas connected by an act of the mind: (3) Every meaningful categorematic word, when used by S, must signify an idea in the mind of S; that idea must either be given immediately in sensation or reflection or constructed out of ideas that have been so given, possibly in conjunction with mental acts.

Locke can say that "real essence," for example, signifies an "idea" in the attenuated sense that it signifies a string of ideas together with acts of the mind: the mentalese for "the real but hidden constitution," etc. So someone who thinks that his word signifies an idea of a real essence is under the impression that he has a single idea adequately representing its object, whereas in fact he has merely a thought of an *x* such that *x*, etc. Locke is able to take over Hobbes's point that some words stand for definite descriptions whose objects are not given in experience while retaining the Port-Royalian insistence that categoremata be correlated with ideas, but he can only do this if he is willing to widen "ideas" to include constructions composed of ideas and acts of the mind.

SUBSTANCE

Perhaps the central test case for (3) is that of substance. For here, if any-where, Locke is in danger of sawing off the branch he sits on. Stillingfleet's insistence that Locke had "almost discarded substance out of the reasonable part of the world"[19] seems justified in light of Locke's consistent attacks on the coherence and intelligibility of the idea of substance in II.xxiii. Like real essence, substance is a "something-I-know-not-what" that must be posited to explain certain features of our experience. My primary concern in this section is not to address the ultimate metaphysical status of substance, al-though my arguments might have consequences for this, but rather to trace out Locke's account of how we generate our idea of substance in the first place.

To begin, we must distinguish three senses of "substance" in Locke's text: we have "substance*s*," which Locke, like the Aristotelians, construes as ordinary middle-sized objects such as people, trees, etc.; "general sub-stances" such as extension and thought as construed by the Cartesians; and

[19] Stillingfleet (1697, p. 234).

finally what Locke calls "pure substance in general." I shall use the word "substance" only in the last sense.

On Locke's view, complex ideas of macro-physical objects must include not only the ideas of the qualities that co-exist in them, but also the obscure and confused idea of substance. Since we cannot imagine how observable qualities could subsist on their own, we must posit something for them to inhere in. It is not enough to say that substance is that which has properties, since properties themselves can have properties. Instead, Locke construes substance as ontologically prior to accidents or modes in that a substance does not require anything further in which to inhere. Locke's account in II.xxiii.1 raised Stillingfleet's ire by suggesting that we form the idea of substance through custom alone rather than reason; Locke says that since we are unable to imagine qualities subsisting on their own, "we accustom our selves, to suppose some *Substratum*, wherein they do subsist, and from which they do result" (II.xxiii.1: 295). This substratum is always something other than all of the observable qualities, including extension. But in his replies to Stillingfleet Locke is at pains to make clear that positing substance is rationally defensible, indeed compulsory; he goes so far as to claim that if he is to be accused of doing away with substance, "Burgersidicius, Sanderson, and the whole tribe of Logicians"[20] must join him in the dock. This seems a bit disingenuous, since traditional Aristotelian logic would not have agreed with Locke that the substance is anything over and above the actual macro-physical object. For them, "substance" must be taken only in the first of the senses discussed above; the role of ultimate subject is played instead by prime matter, which clearly does not meet the traditional Aristotelian requirement of being able to exist as an independent entity. Nevertheless, Locke's demand for an ultimate subject does have an Aristotelian pedigree.

My characterization of Locke's conception of substance is controversial. Michael Ayers has argued that Lockean substance is not an ultimate subject of properties, but is instead simply the real essence thought of under a different concept. To support this, Ayers notes that knowing substance would allow us to explain why the qualities we observe to co-exist do in fact go together, a role also played by real essence. Ayers concludes that "[f]or Locke the real essence simply *is* the internal frame or constitution of the thing."[21] Although the ideas are distinct, their objects have a common explanatory role to play in an ideally completed science, since knowing each

[20] Letter to Stillingfleet, included in the fifth edition of the *Essay* as a footnote to II.xxiii.2.
[21] Ayers (1991, vol. 2, p. 41).

would allow us to explain the co-existence of qualities and properties at the macro-physical level, even if it would not reveal a set of natural kinds to us. One difficulty with Ayers's view is that it neglects the metaphysical role substance must play in addition to its job as the hidden cause of the unity of the qualities we experience. The "support" of properties cannot be read as simply the ultimate "explanation" of why those properties go together. Although this is controversial, Locke's adherence to the traditional model seems to entail that even if we had a God's-eye view and fully knew the real essence, we could *still* sensibly ask what the properties we observe inhere in (see, e.g., II.xxiii.3: 297). If this is true, what E.J. Lowe has called the "sanitized" reading of Locke is untenable.[22]

However that may be, it is clear that sensation and reflection do not provide us with an idea of substance. How, then, can we go about constructing one? I shall argue that Locke in fact offers two slightly different accounts of this process, one involving an appeal to the mental acts and ideas of a definite description, another, to a single complex idea. The former is clearly present in the *Essay*. Locke writes,

So that if anyone will examine himself concerning his *Notion of pure Substance in general*, he will find that he has no other *Idea* of it at all, but only a Supposition of he knows not what support of such Qualities, which are capable of producing simple *Ideas* in us . . . (II.xxiii.2: 295; see II.xxiii.15: 305; I.iv.18: 95)

The only idea we have of substance in general is a supposition of whatever it is that supports the qualities producing the relevant ideas in us. It is revealing that at one point, he writes, "of *Substance*, we have no *Idea* of what it is, but only a confused obscure one of what it does" (II.xiii.19: 175). This, together with his use of the formula "something I know not what," suggests a parallel with Hobbes's position. When speaking in this vein, Locke argues that we in fact have no idea of substance as such;[23] what we have is a supposition of something that fills a certain role, but whose nature remains inaccessible to us.

It is instructive that when Berkeley, anticipating Hume, denies that there is such a thing as mental substance, he attacks precisely the syncategoremata distinctive of definite descriptions. In the *Notebooks*, Berkeley flirts with the notion that the mind is a congeries of perceptions, a position he later rejected. In attacking the substance view, Berkeley writes, "Say you the Mind is not the Perceptions. but that thing wch perceives. I answer you are abus'd by the words that & thing these are vague empty words wthout a meaning"

---

[22] See Lowe (2000).

[23] See also Locke's first entry under "Substance" in his index (1975, p. 745): "S. no Idea of it."

(*PC* 581). Locke's talk of abuse *of* words is replaced by an accusation of abuse *by* words. A definite description account of the meaning of "mind" is allegedly nonsensical because it uses words that lack meaning. This is simply an application of Locke's own ideational argument from nonsense. At this point in his career, Berkeley accepted what he took to be Locke's semiotic empiricism. Later, however, Berkeley rejects semiotic empiricism in the case of words for minds and their acts. In *Alciphron*, Berkeley argues that words that "denote an active principle, soul, or spirit do not, in a strict sense, stand for ideas,"

> And yet they are not insignificant neither; since I understand what is signified by the term *I*, or *myself*, or know what it means, although it be no idea, nor like an idea, but that which thinks, and wills, and apprehends ideas, and operates about them.[24]

Berkeley is here using the very strategy he had earlier condemned.

Although Locke says much in the *Essay* to indicate that he regards "substance" as short for a definite description, it is not obvious that this is his final position. In the exchange with Stillingfleet, for example, he maintains that we can in fact construct an idea of substance that seems not to involve the syncategoremata of a description. Stillingfleet argues that if we have good reason to infer the existence of substance, we must allow that there is an idea of it. Locke replies that there is in fact "a complex idea [of substance], made up of the general idea of something, or being, with the relation of a support to accidents."[25] This account of the idea of substance involves three items: the general idea of "something," the idea of the relation of support, and that of accidents or observable qualities. Without this last element, we have not yet constructed an idea that represents what underlies sensible qualities. Although the idea of being-in-general is the usual focus of criticism, it is well to remember that the relation of support needs ideas of *both* relata.

Locke's vacillation between these two accounts explains his tendency to deny that we have an idea of substance and yet go on talking about "the idea of substance." We need not decide which was his true view, since both accounts run into the same problem, for both require ideas of both being-in-general and support. Can Locke provide them?

No.[26] Given Locke's account of relations, his view cannot even get off the ground. On Locke's view, relations only arise when a *mind* compares two

---

[24] Berkeley, *Alciphron* VII.5, Berkeley (1949–58, vol. 3, p. 292).
[25] Locke (1812, vol. 4, p. 19). For ideas of relations, see III.xxviii.18: 360.
[26] Some of my arguments here draw on E.J. Lowe's (2000).

ideas. Thus relation is "not contained in the real existence of Things, but something extraneous, and superinduced" (II.xxv.8: 322). Relation is only a way of comparing or considering two things (II.xxv.7: 322) and involves an act of the mind. But if this is the case, there is simply no reason to posit a real object to fill the blank spot in the relation of "support." This relation would only appear when a mind considered observable properties together with something else. But since no relation is real, where is the motivation for undertaking an ontological commitment in order to create the second relatum, substance?

This point aside, there is an obvious problem with the idea of being-in-general Locke requires. Recall that in order to generate the idea of substance via the relation of support, we required ideas of both relata. Commentators have focused on the difficulty in filling in the blank, as it were: given that we are aware of qualities, how can we construct an idea of what supports them? But the obverse point also holds. For if we had an idea of being-in-general that fits substance, which does not require anything further in which to inhere, this idea could not be used as the first relatum. It is crucial for Locke's purposes that the idea of being we gain from reflecting on our ideas involve the necessity of being supported or inhering in a further subject. Conversely, the idea of being-in-general we can draw from experience must, it seems, include the notion of being dependent on something for its existence. Given this, it is simply not suited to serve in the construction of an idea of substance.

Lastly, it is far from clear that Locke is entitled to the relevant idea of support. As Berkeley argued, Locke must be using "support" in a metaphorical sense. Experience provides us with instances of support, as when a foundation supports a building. But that is clearly not the requisite idea of support. Locke famously makes fun of the reliance on metaphor in metaphysics while arguing that our idea of substance is obscure. "*Substantia*" we are told "is in plain *English, standing under*, or *upholding*" (II.xxiii.2: 296). If Locke cannot supply a meaning for "support" besides this, Stillingfleet's charge seems justified. When Hylas objects that Philonous has taken his talk of support too literally, Philonous replies,

I am not for imposing any sense on your words: you are at liberty to explain them as you please. But I beseech you, make me understand something by them. You tell me, matter supports or stands under accidents. How! is it as your legs support your body? . . . Pray let me know any sense, literal or not, that you understand it in.[27]

---

[27] *TD* 199; see *TD* 218.

Absent an account of the metaphysical relation of support, Locke must concede that his idea of substance is empty.

Locke's failure to account for our idea of substance can be regarded either as a failure of his philosophy of language in general, which requires us to construct ideas on the basis of experience if our words are to be meaningful, or simply as a failure of Locke's own notion of substance. Like some contemporary metaphysicians,[28] I prefer an account of substance according to which it is not metaphysically distinct from the object itself. The confusion arises when we treat substances and their properties as of the same logical category. It is perfectly possible to say in one logical tone of voice, to borrow a phrase of Ryle's, that substances exist, and in another tone of voice, that properties exist. But we should not take this to mean that the properties require something extra, over and above the object itself, in order to exist. Thus the problem is not semiotic empiricism but rather the particular conception of substance Locke asks us to endorse.

CONCLUSION

We have seen that the distinction between categoremata that signify ideas and those that signify both the contents and acts of the mind that would also be signified by the words of a definite description is central in grasping the extent to which Locke endorses semiotic empiricism. One might plausibly suggest that it is in fact *only* his willingness to countenance such descriptions that prevents the talk of real essence (and perhaps of substance as well) in the *Essay* from itself being accounted gibberish. Despite this innovation, Locke was unable to construct an idea of substance. For unlike real essence, substance is not merely whatever plays a certain explanatory role, but a metaphysical entity Locke invokes to support accidents. Yet it is extremely difficult to see how the relevant ideas of support and being-in-general could be constructed out of materials furnished by experience.

More generally, Locke must modify his linguistic thesis. The slogan "all words stand for ideas" was shown in chapter two to require emendation in order to allow for particles; now it must be further amended to allow for categorematic words that attain their significance not by signifying a single mental object but rather a complex of ideas and mental acts. Correspondingly, Locke's semiotic empiricism is even more permissive than the wide version considered above. This is fully consonant with Locke's larger project of undermining Aristotelianism and making room

---

[28] Esp. Lowe (2000) and perhaps Martin (1980).

for the claims of corpuscular science. His version of the ideational argument from nonsense is designed to be powerful enough to rule out some key claims of Aristotelianism (as we saw in the previous chapter), yet not so powerful that it rules out talk of that which lies beyond experience. In this respect, Locke's handling of the argument from nonsense is a genuine achievement.

CHAPTER 6

The reception of Locke's philosophy of language

With the previous chapters, we have established both the content and the application of Locke's views of language. It is now possible to look at some of the most important reactions to those views, with an eye both to correcting misunderstandings on the part of Locke's respondents and to deepening our grasp of Locke's views themselves.

An exhaustive treatment of this chapter's topic would demand a further monograph. Here, I shall begin by considering two critiques of Locke from his contemporaries (or near-contemporaries) that come from opposite sides of the debate between the Aristotelian and the modern forms of empiricism. Although rarely recognized, Locke's indefatigable Aristotelian critic John Sergeant anticipated many of the most popular objections to Locke's view. Much more often mentioned in this connection is Berkeley; we shall see that his relation to Locke is quite complex, since he seems to misunderstand key parts of Locke's view of language. Exploring Berkeley will also afford us the opportunity to see how the traditional conception of signs sketched above (chapter one) was both exploited and transformed in the modern period.

Next I discuss perhaps the most common source of objections, the privacy of the mental. I distinguish between epistemic and metaphysical versions of the privacy argument. It will emerge that whether Locke can successfully respond to these arguments will turn on his conceptions of mental representation and ostensive definition. In the final chapter, I offer a broader assessment of Locke's overall view from a contemporary perspective.

AN ARISTOTELIAN CRITIQUE: JOHN SERGEANT

Sergeant's official comment on Book III suggests that he thinks Locke's views on language insignificant:

This learned Author having most elaborately, largely and acutely prosecuted in his former Book the distinction of his *Ideas*, and the whole Duty of *Words* being to *signify* our Thoughts to others, I cannot discern what need there could be to take such pains about those Outward Signes.[1]

But this is belied by Sergeant's own practice. In the "second Preliminary" of his *Solid Philosophy*, Sergeant offers a battery of fifteen arguments against Locke, three of which explicitly challenge his views on language.

Contra Locke, Sergeant, as we have seen, holds that what is in the mind in the act of thinking is not an idea or representation but the thing itself. In his ninth argument, Sergeant uses considerations of the nature of language and meaning to support his position: "Notions are the *Meanings*, or (to speak more properly) *what is meant* by the words we use: But *what's meant* by the words is the *Thing it self*; therefore *the Thing it self* is in the Meaning; and consequently in the *Mind*; only which can *mean*."[2] Since only minds are capable of being directed toward objects in an act of thought, and since our words clearly do "mean" the "things themselves," these things must be in the mind. (Sergeant's use of "mean," "signify," and so on, are far from clear, but he certainly uses them as if they meant, at least in part, "refer to." In Sergeant's case, I am happy to admit that Ashworth's understanding of signification might well be correct.) But they are not in the mind materially; things and intentional species are numerically identical on Sergeant's view but have distinct "manners of existence." Unsurprisingly, Locke argues that this is absurd: on his view, Sergeant's direct realism entails that the thing thought of exists materially in the mind. In a letter to Stillingfleet, Locke writes,

For since I make no doubt but that . . . you will allow that you have some immediate objects of your thoughts, which are the materials of that knowledge, about which it is employed, those immediate objects, if they are not, as Mr. J.S. says, the very things themselves, must be ideas. Not thinking your lordship therefore yet so perfect a convert of Mr. J.S.'s, that you are persuaded, that as often as you think of a cathedral church, or of Des Cartes's vortices, that very cathedral church at Worcester or the motion of those vortices, itself exists in your understanding; when one of them never existed but in that one place at Worcester, and the other never existed anywhere in "rerum natura."[3]

Like "Mr. J.S.," Locke requires that the intentional object be ontologically present to the mind (IV.xxi.4: 720–1).[4] For Locke, this means that it makes

---

[1] Sergeant (1984, p. 287).   [2] Sergeant (1984, p. 33).
[3] Locke (1812, vol. 4, pp. 390–1).   [4] See Ayers (1991, vol. 1, chs 5–7).

no sense to say that anything other than an idea can be the immediate object of thought. To Sergeant's claim that the objects' distinct manners of existence do not preclude their numerical identity, Locke argues (in his marginal notes on *Solid Philosophy*) that *a* and *b* cannot have different manners of existence at the same time and still be numerically identical. The indiscernibility of identicals surely rules this out.[5]

Despite the weakness of his own position, Sergeant develops his criticism in his tenth argument. Sergeant points out that "when a Gentleman bids his Servant fetch him a Pint of Wine; he does not mean to bid him fetch the *Idea* of Wine in his own head, but the wine it self which is in the Cellar."[6] If we leave aside Sergeant's metaphysics for a moment, we can see that the kernel of both of these arguments is the intuitive thought that what is meant by a categorematic word is (much of the time) a physical object rather than an idea. Unfortunately, Sergeant has simply misinterpreted Locke's view, just as Mill was to do later (see chapter one); Sergeant's objection tells against the view that words *refer* to ideas, but not the view that words signify ideas, in Locke's sense.

The final argument of Sergeant's we shall examine is stronger. It is worth quoting in full:

> Our words are *ad placitum*, and have no *Natural* Connexion with the Things they signifie, but are order'd to express them by the *Agreement* of Mankind: Therefore what's signified by them, must be *fore-known* to that Agreement. But the *Ideas*, or Resemblances we have, cannot be *fore-known* to this Agreement, since they could not be at all known, (*being in the Mind*,) but by the *Words*; which, not being yet agreed on, can make known, or signifie, nothing. Therefore the *Things* which we naturally had fore-knowledge of, and not the *Ideas*, are that which is signified by *Words*.[7]

Since words, as Locke himself insists, have no natural connection with what they signify, it is only in virtue of the agreement of human beings that they signify anything at all. Sergeant asks, how can this agreement get off the ground? Words are needed only because what lies in each person's mind is hidden, by Locke's own account. But if no one can observe what goes on in another's mind, how can we *agree* to use a given word to signify the same idea? How could we ever check that others were living up their end of the bargain, as it were? Sergeant has neatly turned Locke's own argument from the uses of words against him. Note that Sergeant's argument does not turn

---

[5] I leave aside the question of relative identity, which some might use to defend Sergeant's position.

[6] Sergeant (1984, p. 33).

[7] Sergeant (1984, p. 34). This passage and the preceding ones also lend support to Ashworth's claims about the late Scholastic use of "signification."

on any particular understanding of signification: it is just as strong if we read it as indication, as I have suggested. How can we agree to use words to indicate something of which no two persons could in principle ever be directly aware?

It will already be clear that Locke must deny one of Sergeant's premises. Sergeant's argument only works if he assumes that it is only by means of words that we make our ideas known to others. Locke clearly does not think this is the case. Locke cautions against assuming that other speakers are going along with the "agreement" and recommends that we use ostensive definition, in some cases, to make sure that words are being used in the same sense by different speakers. This move itself, of course, is highly controversial. I discuss Locke's account of ostensive definition below. The concerns Sergeant raises about the privacy of the mental will also be developed and explored below.

A MODERN EMPIRICIST CRITIQUE: GEORGE BERKELEY

According to the orthodox story about Berkeley's development, he began his career as a fervent disciple of Locke's views on language and then rejected them. On this view, although Berkeley in his notebooks endorses Locke's dictum that each significant word stands for an idea, he came to criticize that doctrine in more or less effective ways.

Like many such stories, it is true, so far as it goes. But I want to suggest that the picture is much more complicated. Berkeley was indeed deeply influenced by what he took to be Locke's views, but he was largely mistaken about what those views actually were. What is more, the crucial departure from this early view can be traced to suggestions Locke himself makes, even if Berkeley misunderstands these suggestions. He thus arrives at a view quite dissimilar to Locke's, but he misses some of Locke's most important insights about language.

First I shall explore Berkeley's treatment of signification, arguing that he and Locke understand that notion very differently. I shall then consider the most notable exception to the linguistic thesis, the doctrine of notions. In this section I show how Berkeley arrived at this doctrine partly through a misunderstanding of Locke's discussion of particles in the *Essay*. In the third, I consider Berkeley's position in *Alciphron* on such topics as force and relation, suggesting that his treatment of these topics does not constitute an exception to the linguistic thesis, as Berkeley understood it. It will emerge that Berkeley was neither so successful in overthrowing, nor so acute in understanding, Locke as is usually imagined.

BERKELEY AND THE LINGUISTIC THESIS

I wish to begin by setting out two Lockean propositions, leaving open for now the precise sense in which Berkeley understands them:
(1) The purpose of language is to communicate ideas.
(2) All significant words stand for (i.e., are signs of) ideas.

In the *Notebooks*, Berkeley often endorses (2) (*PC* 356, 378, 422), but each of these entries is marked with a "+," probably indicating that it was to be discarded. In *PI*, Berkeley traces the hated doctrine of abstract ideas to the conjunction of (1) and (2):

But to give a farther account how words came to produce the doctrine of abstract ideas, it must be observed that it is a received opinion, that language has no other end but the communicating our ideas, and that every significant name stands for an idea. This being so, and it being withal certain, that names, which yet are not thought altogether insignificant, do not always mark out particular conceivable ideas, it is straightaway concluded that they stand for abstract notions. (*PI* 19)

On Berkeley's account, if we accept (1) and (2), and add "what nobody will deny," viz., that there are some words that do not always suggest particular determinate ideas, we will be driven to posit abstract ideas as the significates of those words. It is not clear how this argument is supposed to work. For, as we shall see, the doctrine of abstract ideas is traced most plausibly to the doctrine that each word must always signify *the same* idea in order to be univocal. The counterexamples Berkeley has in mind in the final sentence above involve, not words that do not signify ideas, but words that signify no *particular* idea but any one of a given class of ideas indifferently. It is thus a bit misleading for Berkeley to present his case as he does, since (1) and (2) are not the real targets he has in view.

It is crucial that Berkeley is not suggesting here that there are significant words that are *never* associated with an idea. On Berkeley's own account, a word becomes general, not by signifying a single general idea, but simply through its capacity to suggest to the mind any number of ideas indifferently. This is not to deny (2). Even though "there is no such thing as one precise and definite signification annexed to any general name" (*PI* 18), it remains the case, for all Berkeley has said so far in *PI*, that such names must suggest ideas to the mind. Berkeley continues:

And a little attention will discover, that it is not necessary (even in the strictest reasonings) significant names which stand for ideas should, every time they are used, excite in the understanding the ideas they are made to stand for: in reading and discoursing, names being for the most part used as letters are in *algebra*, in which though a particular quantity be marked by each letter, yet to proceed right it is not requisite that in every step each letter suggest to your thoughts, that particular quantity it was appointed to stand for. (*PI* 19)

Molyneux wrote Berkeley to ask the natural question: if we allow ourselves to reason without ideas, at least sometimes, what guarantees that we stay on the right track? How can we ensure that our reasonings are sound without employing the ideas at every step? Berkeley's response relies on the formal character of inference: we can be sure of this so long as we are manipulating symbols according to the rules prescribed by logic and grammar. Berkeley writes, "I cannot but dissent from what You say, of there being no set Rules for the Ranging and Disposition of Words but only the Syllogistic, for to Me it appears That all Grammar & every part of Logic contain little else than Rules for Discourse & Ratiocination by Words."[8] Moreover, in order to observe these rules, it is not necessary to check the words against the ideas in question at each step: since the rules are purely formal, attending to the moves made with the counters will suffice.

This leads to a modification of (2):

(3) All significant words must be able to suggest an idea to the mind.

This dispositional claim is more plausible than (2). But it is still true that there must be some idea or other that we can call up and associate with a given word. The only exception to (2) is provided by the doctrine of notions, to which I turn below. Let us now look at Berkeley's treatment of (1).

In *PI* 20, Berkeley objects to (1): "[T]he communicating of ideas marked by words is not the chief and only end of language." Language has many other purposes, including the raising of passions or the direction of another's actions. In *PC*, Berkeley made this point explicitly with regard to religious language:

When I say I will reject all Propositions wherein I know not fully & adequately & clearly so far as knowable the Thing meant thereby This is not to be extended to propositions in the Scripture. I speak of Matters of Reason & Philosophy not Revelation, In this I think an Humble Implicit faith becomes us just (where we cannot comprehend & Understand the proposition) such as a popish peasant gives to propositions he hears at Mass in Latin. (*PC* 720)

A similar thought is presented in the so-called First Sermon, when Berkeley discusses the description of the rewards of heaven: "'tis wt eye hath not seen nor ear heard neither hath it enter'd into the heart of man to conceive."[9]

---

[8] Letter 6 in Berkeley (1949–58, vol. 8, p. 27).   [9] Berkeley (1949–58, vol. 1, p. 12).

This text was to recur as an example of useful discourse not associated with ideas throughout Berkeley's writings, and the example of a promise of a "good thing" in *PI* 20 clearly echoes it. In these passages, Berkeley presents a noncognitive analysis of at least some religious discourse, surprising in the works of one who was to become a bishop. As Antony Flew points out, "neither [Berkeley], nor any other bishop of his century, would have had any truck with a religion without propositions."[10] According to Berkeley, there clearly are cognitive regions of such discourse (roughly, those falling under the heading of "natural" as opposed to "revealed" religion). Nevertheless religion includes mysterious pronouncements that perform an emotive or prescriptive function, rather than a fact-stating one. Note that, unlike the emotive words discussed in *PI*, the propositions in Scripture are compared to propositions in an unknown language. In *PI*, the suggestion was that words that were once associated with ideas come to excite emotions directly, without the intervention of those ideas. But here Berkeley suggests that there need be no such initial ideational link.

Although Berkeley presents his account of the emotive and prescriptive uses of language in the context of an attack on both (1) and (2), it should be clear that it says nothing whatever about (2). Thus Luce and Jessop are wrong when they say in a note that the biblical text in the First Sermon "supplied Berkeley with a decisive argument against Locke's principle that every significant name must stand for an idea."[11] If "significant" here means "signifying an idea," or, more generally, "contributing to the fact-stating uses of language," then the text in question is not a counterexample at all. This is not the role Berkeley sees such language as playing. If "significant" means something else, such as "useful" or "able to evoke emotion," then the text in no way conflicts with (2). Berkeley does speak in *PI* 19 of "significant names that stand for ideas," suggesting that he intends a contrast with other kinds of significant names that do not. But Berkeley is careful in *PI* 20 not to say that the words used emotively or prescriptively are significant. In *ALC*, Euphranor says that a discourse "that directs how to act or excites to the doing or forbearance of an action may, it seems, be useful and significant, although the words whereof it is composed should not bring each a distinct idea into our minds."[12] Here "significant" seems intended as an honorific – it is to be contrasted with "useless." In this sense Berkeley might well claim that prescriptive or emotive discourse is significant, but this, obviously, would not be to disagree with the claim that such discourse is nevertheless non-cognitive.

---

[10] Flew (1993, p. 223).   [11] In Berkeley (1949–58, vol. 1, p. 12).   [12] *ALC* VII.5, p. 292.

It is not clear how damaging the denial of (1) is to Locke's own position. Locke may simply have neglected uses of language other than descriptive or cognitive ones; this shows his account of language to be incomplete but not fatally flawed. That Locke is guilty as charged appears from such claims as this: "When a Man speaks to another, it is that he may be understood; and the end of Speech is, that those Sounds, as Marks, may make known his *Ideas* to the Hearer" (III.ii.2: 405). This is clearly false, and Berkeley takes Locke to task for this in a number of places.[13] In fact, the neglect of other uses of language seems to be a recurring and recalcitrant malaise in philosophy of language generally. Thus J.O. Urmson can say of logical atomism that it "regarded [other uses of language besides descriptive statements] as beneath philosophical notice . . . [a]s for the subtlety of the distinction between giving verdicts, telling stories, making claims, consolation, congratulation, promising, all this was hidden by the blindness which is the guardian angel of preconceptions."[14] This blindness obscured not only emotive uses of language but also its uses in illocutionary acts, such as promising, warning, and so on. Yet obviously one might reject (1) and simply amend (3) to read:

(4) In all descriptive uses of language, all significant words must be able to suggest an idea to the mind, though they need not do so on each occasion.

This retains the kernel of (2). Berkeley's allegiance to (4) is suggested at the end of *PI*, where he announces that he will endeavor to take the ideas themselves (rather than the words) "bare and naked in my view" (*PI* 21) and enjoins the reader to do the same (*PI* 25; cp. Locke's *Essay* II.x.21). At least in *PI*, then, what we have is not a wholesale rejection of the Lockean position but three revisions of it: words need not suggest the same idea on each occasion of use or to each auditor in order to be used univocally; the purpose of language is not confined to communication of ideas; even when such communication is intended, one need not have an occurrent idea associated with each word, even though, in descriptive discourse, such an association must be at least possible.

But I have left unclear what this association consists in, which Berkeley, like Locke, speaks of as "signifying" or "standing for." The clearest discussion of this concept comes in *TVV*. In general, a sign is something that suggests something else to the mind. In the quotations from Berkeley above, we see that he often speaks of a word's "exciting" an idea in the mind of the speaker, or "suggesting" it. In *TVV*, he distinguishes between arbitrary

---

[13] E.g., *PC* 720; *P* 20; the so-called "First Sermon" (1949–58, vol. 1, pp. 11–13); and *ALC* VII.10.
[14] Urmson (1967, pp. 197–8).

and necessary signification. Cases of the latter include a similarity between ideas (as the mind passes from an idea to another that resembles it) or causality (as when the mind infers from the effect to the cause or *vice versa*). An idea of sensation is an indication of God's existence, since it is a "sign or effect" (*P* 148) of God's power.

But even when "there is no such relation of similitude or causality, nor any necessary connexion whatsoever, two things, by their mere coexistence, or two ideas, merely by being perceived together, may suggest or signify one the other, their connexion being all the while arbitrary; for it is the connexion only, as such, that causeth this effect" (*TVV* 39). Berkeley here exploits the ancient notion of reminiscent signification (see chapter one above), just as in the case of ideas of sensation he exploited that of indicative signification. A great number of reminiscent signs constitute a language (*TVV* 40); this language can be instituted either by human beings or by God. Indeed it is one of Berkeley's central claims that visual ideas constitute a divine language. There is thus no difference in kind between words and visual ideas considered as means of communication. The similarity goes even deeper, since we master each system of signs in the same way: "by a connexion taught us by experience, [visible ideas] come to signify and suggest [the sensations attending vision] to us, after the same manner that words of any language suggest the ideas they are made to stand for" (*P* 43). The person born blind and then made to see is in the same position as a monolingual Francophone who is suddenly plopped down in Tennessee.

When pressing these points of similarity between human and divine language (as in *ALC* IV.10 and *P* 44), Berkeley forgets his criticism of (1). Thus in *NTV* he writes,

Upon the whole, I think we may fairly conclude that the proper objects of vision constitute an universal language of the Author of Nature, whereby we are instructed how to regulate our actions in order to attain those things that are necessary to the preservation and well-being of our bodies, as also to avoid whatever may be hurtful and destructive of them . . . And *the manner wherein they signify and mark unto us the objects which are at a distance is the same with that of languages and signs of human appointment*, which do not suggest the things signified by any likeness or identity of nature, but only by an habitual connexion that experience has made us observe between them" (*NTV* 147, emphasis added; see *ALC* IV.8).

My habit of moving from the sound "tree" to the idea of a tree is so entrenched that it takes some effort to see that it is happening. The arbitrary connection is purely the product of a habit I acquired when first learning English. Berkeley's position here is not obviously consistent with (4), or with the rejection of (1), since it seems to assume that a word is significant only on those occasions when it does in fact elicit the proper idea. Moreover, no provision is made, even in the late *ALC* text cited above, for notions. Let us take up each issue in turn.

When drawing the comparison with the divine language, Berkeley implies that words, like visual ideas, were instituted in order to cause a certain idea to occur in the mind. In the case of words, their purpose is to allow a speaker to cause his hearer to have a certain idea. This seems to support (2) rather than (4): if a word is to be significant, must it not raise, and not merely be able to raise, an idea in the mind of the hearer? Compare the divine language. There the claim is not simply that one is able to associate an idea with a given visual impression, but that one in fact does so as the result of habit.

Yet perhaps this is a cavil. Berkeley might well insist on the analogy between human and divine language and deny that a proposition analogous to (4) holds true for the latter. Berkeley's rejection of (1), however, seems a more difficult position to accommodate in light of his remarks on the nature of language as such. For there is nothing analogous to an emotive or prescriptive use of visual ideas. But again, Berkeley can parry this objection. His claim is that visual ideas and words are alike in that they arbitrarily signify other ideas; human language has a further use that the divine language does not. Alternatively, Berkeley might claim that the divine language does have at least prescriptive uses. This is not obviously absurd, though I will not press the point.

The only real difficulty raised by these passages, I think, is that they leave little room for notions. Words for active beings are supposed to be significant even though they cannot be linked with any idea. It is not just that the analogy between visual ideas and words breaks down at this point. It is rather that Berkeley's remarks in the context of the divine language lead him to pronouncements that are not consistent with his overall view. The italicized portion of the above passage makes this particularly evident. And later on in that work Berkeley will give perhaps his clearest statement of the doctrine of notions.

I will pursue this issue in the next section. Now, let us ask how well Berkeley has understood Locke. As we have seen, Locke's view is that words signify ideas in the mind of the *speaker*, not the hearer. Berkeley recognizes this in *PI*, where he characterizes his opponent as holding that general names are significant when the speaker designs them "for marks of ideas in his own [mind], which he would have them raise in the mind of the hearer" (*PI* 20; Locke himself uses "mark" and "sign" interchangeably; see III.ii.1–2). But more often he characterizes Locke simply as endorsing (2), with signification understood as suggesting or exciting an idea. Thus the clearly Lockean Alciphron is made to say, "Words are signs: they do or should stand for ideas, which so far as they suggest they are significant."[15] Alciphron's position then is one according to which significant words are those that summon a certain idea in the listener. The arguments of previous chapters have shown that this position is not Locke's. Although Locke grants that in practice much of the time we simply allow ourselves to have ideas caused by another's speech, he never calls this relation between word and idea *signification*. Moreover, as we have seen, this causal connection is parasitic on the initial connection of indicative signification. If I did not at one time infer that your word *x* indicated that you were having idea *y*, your utterance of *x* would never come to be associated in my mind with *y*. The difference between Locke and Berkeley here roughly maps onto the difference between indicative and reminiscent signification, drawn explicitly by Sextus Empiricus and, later, Gassendi (see above, chapter two).

This distinction makes available to Locke an argument against (4). The argument concerns how the signification relation is set up in the first place. In the case of the visual language, Berkeley can plausibly claim that experience creates an association between two ideas such that one leads the mind to think of the other. But human language is crucially different, since it is conventional. How can we have an experience of the idea with which a speaker wishes to associate a given word? On Locke's view, the role of words in causing us automatically to think of ideas is parasitic on their role as indicative signs of those ideas. The latter relation needs to be consciously instituted, by means of ostensive definition, for example, before words can "suggest" or "excite" ideas in the hearer (see IV.xviii.3: 689). The challenge to Berkeley is to explain *how* the reminiscent signification relation comes into existence in the first place. With the visual language, as I have suggested, we can easily see how this works. But a language that depends on human convention seems to require a very different basis.

NOTIONS

I have been arguing that Locke and Berkeley usually use "sign" in different senses. Thus Berkeley's debt to Locke is complicated by the fact that he understood "sign" in a very different way. Indeed, Locke would have found Berkeley's position deeply problematic. He would have seen Berkeley's view as conceptually impossible, given that language is an arbitrary human construction.

---

[15] *ALC* VII.2, p. 287.

Does Berkeley's attack in *PI*, then, miss its target? Clearly (1) is indifferent among different understandings of signification. (2), however, is not. We must conclude that Berkeley has simply misunderstood Locke. Locke is not saying that each time a word is spoken, it must excite the proper idea in the mind of the hearer in order to be significant. Rather, his position is that significant words are those that indicate the proper ideas in the mind of the speaker.

One might well argue that this difference is not so great as it at first appears. For Locke is still claiming that the distinction between significant and insignificant descriptive speech is to be drawn in ideational terms. That is, Locke still requires an idea to be associated (in a sense neutral between the two kinds of signification) with a given word in order for it to be significant. This is not correct, however, since Locke believes there are some words, namely particles, that signify mental acts rather than ideas (see above, chapter two). The slogan "all words signify ideas," although it occurs often enough in varying forms in the early parts of Book III, must be relaxed to accommodate particles. Thus Berkeley's *Alciphron* gives an incomplete, and to that extent, uncharitable presentation of Locke's view. Locke simply does not hold (2). Berkeley might be forgiven some imprecision in his statement of Locke's thesis. Berkeley often characterizes the opposing position as one according to which *names*, rather than words generally, signify ideas (see, e.g., *PI* 19).

What is interesting here is that these passages about particles in the *Essay* provided, ironically, the impetus for what is in some ways Berkeley's most significant departure from the Lockean theses (1)–(4): the doctrine of notions. Berkeley's doctrine allows what Locke's cannot: a significant categorematic word that cannot be associated with any idea.

In his first notebook, Berkeley claims that "soul" or mind signifies "one Complex idea made up of existence, willing & perception in a large sense" (*PC* 154; cp. *PC* 44). In the second notebook, however, Berkeley becomes suspicious of abstract ideas such as "existence," which "is never thought of by the Vulgar" (*PC* 552). He thus feels compelled to jettison his earlier account. He writes:

Consult, ransack yr Understanding wt find you there besides several perceptions or thoughts. Wt mean you by the word mind you must mean something that you perceive or yt you do not perceive, a thing not perceived is a contradiction. to mean (also) a thing you do not perceive is a contradiction. We are all in this matter strangely abused by words. (*PC* 579)

Mind is a congeries of Perceptions. Take away Perceptions & you take away the Mind put the Perceptions & you put the Mind. (*PC* 580)

In *PC* 579 we can see Berkeley struggling to accommodate knowledge of the mind within the confines presented by the principle that all knowledge is only of ideas (*PC* 522). In these passages, Berkeley suggests that if the mind cannot be known by means of an idea, it cannot be perceived at all, which makes the mind "a contradiction," just as much as unperceived matter. In a note on the verso page, Berkeley suggests that we do not know the mind at all; "this will be plain if we examine wt we mean by the word knowledge" (*PC* 576a). What Berkeley requires is a means of thinking about and knowing the mind that does not involve ideas. He found this by reflecting on Locke's position on particles.

Berkeley writes, "The Understanding seemeth not to differ from its perceptions or Ideas. Qu: wt must one think of the Will & passions" (*PC* 587). The will is essentially active and therefore there can be no idea of it, since ideas are passive (*PC* 643, 657). But at *PC* 639, Berkeley claims that it is demonstrable that "a Man can never be brought to Imagine any thing should exist whereof he has no Idea. Whoever says he does, banters himself with Words." Berkeley requires words for the will or volition that are not associated with ideas and yet are significant (in the cognitive sense). Locke, as Berkeley seems to have come to realize, had already made room for such words in his discussion of particles. Berkeley writes: "Some words there are wch do not stand for Ideas v.g. particles Will etc." (*PC* 661).

Locke of course did not claim that particles stand for volitions, but for the mental operations necessary to unite ideas into propositions and propositions into senseful discourse. Berkeley, however, takes mental operations and volitions to be equivalent: "Tis allow'd that Particles stand not for Ideas & yet they are not said to be empty useless sounds. The truth on't is they stand for the operations of the mind i.e. volitions." (*PC* 667).

The escape route from the narrow confines of (1) is provided by Locke himself. What was in Locke's hands a way of accounting for propositional content and the logical relations among propositions becomes in Berkeley's a way of accounting for discourse of the mind. What the two uses have in common is that in neither case is there an idea lying behind the word.

Berkeley did not use the claim that words might be associated with acts of the mind in order to account for significant discourse about minds alone. Words for relations must also be associated with acts of the mind rather than ideas:

We may be said to have some knowledge or notion of our own minds, of spirits and active beings, whereof in a strict sense we have not ideas. In like manner we know and have a notion of relations between things or ideas, which relations are distinct from the ideas or things related, inasmuch as the latter may be perceived by us without perceiving the former. (*P* 89)

It is also to be remarked, that all relations including an act of the mind, we cannot so properly be said to have an idea, but rather a notion of the relations or habitudes between things. (*P* 142)

On Locke's view, ideas of relations always involve mental acts. Such an idea "consists in the consideration and comparing one *Idea* with another" (II.xii.7: 166; see II.xxv.5: 321). If we wish to distinguish between ideas and mental acts and operations, it seems odd to class thoughts of relations so understood among the former rather than the latter. Berkeley insists on a mild reform of Locke's mental taxonomy when he writes, "[t]o me it seems that ideas, spirits and relations are all in their respective kinds, the object of human knowledge and subject of discourse: and that the term *idea* would be improperly extended to signify everything we know or have any notion of" (*P* 89), even if "this is after all an affair of verbal concern" (*P* 142).

Despite appearances, then, Berkeley and Locke agree on:

(5) In all descriptive uses of language, all significant words must signify either an idea or an act of the mind, or a complex of both.

But here again we run into a problem with Berkeley's conception of linguistic signification. If words signify mental acts, it must be indicative signification that is at issue: they indicate to the hearer that the speaker is performing a certain mental operation. It seems very odd to say that words might excite or cause such a mental act in the mind of the hearer, even if they might suggest the *idea* of that act. Moreover, Berkeley's official accounts of language on analogy with visual ideas seem to have no room for words that indicate rather than suggest or excite.

FORCE AND MOTION

We have seen that although Locke is committed to (1), he does not endorse (2). And even allowing for the string of revisions above, Locke does not endorse (5) as Berkeley understands it. We must conclude, then, that where (2) and its successors are involved, Locke and Berkeley are simply talking past each other. Berkeley's attack on (1) is well taken, but it hardly amounts to a devastating critique.

But there is another way in which the two might be brought into direct disagreement. Let us revise (5) so as to be neutral between the different conceptions' signification:

(6) In all descriptive uses of language, all significant words must be associated with either an idea or an act of the mind, or a complex of both.

Here, "association" means signification in either of the two senses and does not require that on each occasion of use the associated idea or act must be present. Locke and Berkeley both accept (6). The differences only emerge when we attempt to cash out "association." For the two have distinct conceptions of the relation of signification.

By contrast, Antony Flew has claimed that in *ALC* Berkeley extends "indefinitely the list of words that do not, and perhaps cannot, stand for ideas."[16] Flew points out that in *ALC* Berkeley includes not just notions and relations but concepts such as force and grace. Such concepts can figure in true propositions, and thus belong under the heading of descriptive or fact-stating uses of language, although they cannot be associated with any idea. Indeed, Flew wants to go further and claim that they cannot be associated with any idea or mental act. Berkeley, on Flew's view, has anticipated Wittgenstein's dictum that use rather than private mental object or event is responsible for meaning.

But it is not at all clear that Berkeley does wish to class propositions involving such terms as "force" with descriptive uses. I shall argue that Flew goes wrong in neglecting Berkeley's instrumentalist conception of science. For Flew distinguishes between the theoretical and the practical uses of language, and claims, *contra* Bennett, that the former involves words that cannot be associated with ideas. Although this is true enough, it does not prove Flew's point, since for Berkeley, as we shall see, theoretical discourse itself is at bottom practical.

In *ALC* VII, Berkeley draws an analogy between force and grace: Euphranor need not adduce an idea that can be associated with the latter, since even Alciphron must agree that there is no such idea associated with some of the fundamental notions of science. There may be "divers true and useful propositions concerning the one [grace] as well as the other [force]."[17] What is it for such a proposition to be true? It is vital to see that there are two ways of taking any proposition involving such terms: as predicating something, a power or quality, such as force or grace, of the subject; or as tools for predicting events or influencing behavior. Berkeley, of course, denies that the former is the proper way to understand such propositions. Euphranor asks Alciphron to consider "force itself in its own precise idea," abstracting it from its effects, such as motion. Unsurprisingly, this proves impossible. Nevertheless, Euphranor argues that there are "evident propositions or theorems relating to force, which contain useful truths."[18] Yet the truth of such propositions does not consist in their accurately depicting the world. A proposition such as "a body with conjunct

---

[16] Flew (1993, p. 222).   [17] *ALC* VII.7, p. 296.   [18] *ALC* VII.7, p. 295.

forces describes the diagonal of a parallelogram, in the same time that it would the sides with separate" (*ibid.*) does not tell us about the world but guides our calculations and actions. Berkeley uses the same example in *De Motu*, where he argues that such propositions are "of service to reckoning and mathematical demonstrations"; but this "is one thing, to set forth the nature of things is another" (*De Motu* 18). Here Flew might well argue that the usefulness of these propositions does not prevent their also having a descriptive role; this seems to be Flew's main point against Bennett.[19] But everything Berkeley says points to the conclusion that the practical use of these propositions does indeed exhaust their "significance." "*Force, gravity, attraction*, and terms of this sort are useful for reasonings and reckonings about motion and bodies in motion, but not for understanding the simple nature of motion itself or for indicating so many distinct qualities" (*De Motu* 17). The theoretical, for Berkeley, is no less practical than the emotive.

Berkeley's "revolutionary insight," then, is not to shift the burden of the meaningfulness of descriptive language in these cases from "the (private) idea to the (public) use"[20] but instead to widen the class of non-descriptive or practical "meanings" to include not just emotive uses but theoretical as well. The ontological commitments of science are avoided by recasting science itself in instrumentalist terms, not by carving out a new realm of descriptive meanings that have no links to mental acts and objects. This conception of science is indeed revolutionary. But Berkeley achieves it by in effect divorcing the theoretical uses of language from the descriptive. Such claims are only apparently engaged in describing "the nature of things." When we miss this, we bog down in the fruitless search for the nature of force or motion in itself.

If I am right, the relation between Locke and Berkeley on language is quite complex. Where Berkeley does disagree with Locke, he is following up Locke's own insights, although he does so in a way Locke himself would not welcome. The exception here is the case of the theoretical uses of language. But Berkeley does not, as we have seen, depart from Locke's general principle that each significant word in descriptive discourse must be associated with either an act of the mind or an idea. Instead he removes the propositions of science from descriptive discourse altogether.

PRIVACY: EPISTEMIC ISSUES

We have seen that Locke requires us to infer on the basis of a sign (a word) what is happening in a speaker's mind if we are to understand

---

[19] See Flew (1993, p. 222).   [20] Flew (1993, p. 216).

what is said. How could we ever know whether our inferences are justified, or yield a true conclusion? How can we know if our interlocutors understand us, or we, them? It seems we can never know whether or not we "speak two Languages" (III.ii.4: 407), since we can never be sure that speaker and hearer are annexing the same idea (or mental act) to a given word. It is important to note at the start that Locke accepts that *if* we are annexing different ideas to the same word, we cannot communicate: "[I]f it should happen, that any two thinking Men should really have different *Ideas*, I do not see how they could discourse or argue one with another" (II.xiii.27: 180).

In this, Locke agrees with Frege, who argues that if the objects of thought are different, disagreement becomes impossible: "If [someone holding the view that thoughts are ideas] heard from me the opinion that a thought is not an idea he could not dispute it, for, indeed, it would not now concern him."[21] Just as one who says, "I washed my car yesterday" does not disagree with one who says, "I did not wash my car yesterday," two speakers annexing different ideas to the same word are incapable of disagreement.

The complaint that we can never know whether our sign-inference is correct is a standard one, lodged by, among others, Bennett, Stephen Land, and Robert Hanna.[22] It probably has its origins in the work of Frege and Wittgenstein, even if they do not explicitly target Locke.[23]

But the objection ignores much of what Locke has to say. In the first place, Locke is aware of the skeptical consequences of his view and counsels epistemic humility when judging whether communication is actually taking place or not, i.e., whether we are actually annexing the same idea to a given word (see, e.g., II.xxxii.9: 386).[24] More important, it ignores Locke's remedies for this predicament.[25]

Locke says that our ideas, when referred to those in other men's minds (i.e., supposed to be conformable to them) "*may any of them be false*" (II.xxxii.9: 386). Some of our ideas have a "standard . . . in Nature" (III.ix.5: 477) whereby the signification of our words may be checked. The "only sure way" words for our simple ideas of sensation, for example, can have

---

[21] "Thoughts," in Frege (1977, p. 17).
[22] They do not put the criticism in these terms. For Land, see his (1986, pp. 35–41); for Robert Hanna, see his (1991, p. 795).
[23] Thus Land cites *Philosophical Investigations* I §377 for support.
[24] See chapter four for a treatment of the "secret references." Here it is important to see that the skeptical consequences Locke approves are not global, but merely local. That is, he *does* believe there is a way to be sure that we are using the same word for the same idea; his counsel is against assuming this to be so.
[25] For more on Locke's "rectification of names" (III.ix.7: 478), see Losonsky (1994) and Aarsleff (1964).

their significations settled is "*by presenting to his* [the person one would teach] *Senses that Subject, which may produce it in his Mind*, and make him actually have the *Idea*, that Word stands for" (III.xi.14: 515).

When some simple ideas are conjoined in our experience, we can say that nature provides a standard by which to settle the signification of a word for a complex idea composed of those simple ones. But in the case of mixed modes, this usually is not the case; any complex ideas that the mind "makes at pleasure" (II.ix.7: 478) lack standards in nature. The best that can be done here is to ostensively define, if possible, the constituent simple ideas.

Many writers, from Augustine to Wittgenstein and Quine,[26] have claimed that ostensive definition radically underdetermines reference. When I place a red ball before someone, to which of the many ideas caused by it am I directing his attention? If I try to define "round" in this way, what makes it the case that the student will not instead annex the idea of redness to that word? To take a particular case: Quine argues that in cases of terms with "divided reference" (as opposed to mass terms like "water"), ostension does not fix reference. This is because with a term such as "rabbit" one must master "its principle of individuation: where one rabbit leaves off and another begins." *Pace* Wittgenstein, Quine grants that mass terms can be mastered by ordinary processes of conditioning and induction, even if this may take many lessons. It is only when questions of individuation arise that ostension underdetermines reference. When translating a foreign tongue, for example, Quine argues that we will find many competing hypotheses equally confirmed by the facts of language use. The fact that the natives use "gavagai" while pointing to rabbits does not itself tell us whether they are referring to rabbits or undetached rabbit parts, or rabbit stages, or what have you. Quine's argument for the indeterminacy of reference is sometimes seen as an objection to mentalism (the doctrine that mental states fix reference). I do not think we can accuse Quine himself of this confusion; he clearly assumes that mentalism is false from the outset. For Quine, only behavioral evidence is to be admitted in fixing reference, even in one's own.[27]

There is an enormous literature attempting to refute this Quinean thesis, which I shall not repeat here.[28] Let me instead develop what I think is the most natural reply. If Quine's argument works, it works not just for

---

[26] See Augustine, *De Magistro* 10.35ff.; Wittgenstein's *Philosophical Investigations* I §§27–34 and Quine (1969).

[27] Quine (1969, pp. 26–9).

[28] See, e.g., Levin (1971). My brief reply draws on Searle (1987), esp. pp. 130–3.

our translations of foreign languages, but for own language. (Quine and Davidson, incidentally, both seem happy with this consequence.) This entails that there is *for us* no way to tell what we mean by "rabbit." In this, John Searle finds a *reductio ad absurdum* of Quine's linguistic behaviorism: if meaning is (eliminatively) reduced to correlations between external stimuli and dispositions to verbal behavior, our words have no determinate reference. But we do know what we mean by our own words; "rabbit" in English does refer to rabbits as opposed to undetached rabbit parts. So linguistic behaviorism must be false. Another way to put this point is that the argument itself presupposes that we know at least in our own case the difference between referring to rabbits and referring to rabbit-stages. But if behavioral evidence does not fix reference for speakers of "Gavagai"-talk, it does not do so in our case either. So the argument has to assume the very fact that it calls into question, viz., that we know what we mean by our own words.

Quine sees that his thesis tends toward this conclusion.[29] His solution is to advert to the relativity of reference: seen against a background language, reference is determinate. We English speakers can be said to refer to rabbits by "acquiescing in our mother tongue and taking its words at face value."[30] Is Quine entitled to this acquiescence? After all, our mother tongue on his account is itself just a set of dispositions to verbal behavior (in response to "surface irritations"). We can't take our own language "at face value" because by Quine's own argument there is no fact of the matter about what that value is. Quine's position can be regarded not as an intriguing and important result but rather as a *reductio* of linguistic behaviorism. In any case, it cannot be seen as posing a genuine threat to Locke's views on ostensive definition since it simply assumes from the start that Locke's view is false.

In general, I think that philosophers tend to exaggerate the degree to which ostension underdetermines reference, and to ignore the possibility of correcting error by future instances of ostension. I believe that Quine's claim with regard to mass terms, namely, that the only difficulty attaching to the ostensive definition of terms is that of any induction, holds for language generally. Philosophers have tended to abstract from the context in which ostensive definition is apt, in the real world, to be performed. Teacher and student are not in a vacuum: they have come to this point because of their combined interests, intentions, and goals, and they might well have behind

---

[29] See Quine (1969, pp. 47–8).   [30] Quine (1969, p. 49).

them a history of other acts of ostension.[31] All of this helps to make the referent of the ostensive act determinate.

Even granting the ability of ostensive definition to determine which idea is signified by a word that refers (in Locke's attenuated sense) to a physical object, however, it is very hard to see how it can help us fix the signification of particles. For these indicate acts in the mind of the speaker, which, it seems, could never be the objects of ostensive definition. Locke seems to see this when he grants that most of our words for the operations of the mind, and indeed almost all our words for non-sensible things, had as their "primary signification" (here, original acceptation) simple ideas of sense. These then are "*transferred to more abstruse significations*" (III.i.5: 403), but Locke does not say much more. His thought apparently is that it is their metaphorical relation with non-sensible things that allows these simple ideas to play the role they do. But the sense of a metaphor, it seems, is parasitic on the literal senses of the words involved; one must grasp the latter before being in a position to grasp the former. Since I am acquainted with the acts of my own mind through ideas of reflection, there seems to be no problem in making this transfer intra-subjectively. The problem comes when we try to calibrate our words for mental operations; since ostensive definition cannot be invoked, we must hope that others have picked up on the metaphorical relation. But it is unclear how, on Locke's own terms, we could ever check that this is in fact the case.

PRIVACY: METAPHYSICAL ISSUES

The difficulties just discussed are apt to be lumped in with difficulties of a quite different kind. For in addition to asking, how do we *know* that we are annexing the same idea to a given word, we can also ask, can these ideas be the same? The question is not whether our ideas in this or that circumstance can be the same, but rather, whether it even makes sense to talk of two ideas in different minds being the same. For if our words signify ideas, which are private entities, it is hard to see how we could ever succeed in talking *about* the same thing. Put more perspicuously, Locke's account

---

[31] For example, imagine a case in which a child learns the word "dog" through ostension. Suppose that the child and dog have been interacting; the parent then says "dog" and points at the dog. Why should we think it mysterious that the child has a good chance of learning the word "dog" in this way? Naturally, this account assumes that the child has some pre-linguistic ability to respond differentially to objects. I argue above that Locke can posit such an ability without violating his empiricism. For more on the question of pre-linguistic capacities for carving up one's environment, in both human and non-human animals, see Alasdair MacIntyre (1999).

of language threatens to strip us of our ability to affirm or deny the same proposition, or to talk about the same thing.

These worries are raised most clearly by Frege. Though Frege does not explicitly mention Locke as one of his targets, Locke is clearly a member of the empiricist tradition Frege attacks. It is worthwhile, then, to see whether Frege's criticisms can be made to tell against Locke's position as I have stated it. I am interested here in a particular strand of Frege's anti-psychologistic arguments; I do not pretend to have addressed all such strands.

A good way into these issues is to take up the inverted spectrum problem.[32] This is usually posed in an epistemic form: "how could I ever know that anyone else is having the same internal experiences as I am? In particular, how could I ever know that you are using "blue" to signify the same idea as I?" Locke's response is in effect to change the question to "what are the criteria for sameness of idea?" Once we answer this question, the initial problem takes on an entirely new light.

I have developed a Lockean account of "significative" sameness, whereby what determines the sameness of two ideas is not a similarity between their introspectible contents but rather their epistemic roles, which in turn are founded on their *causal* roles. Two ideas are the "same," on this view, if they are evidence for the presence of the extra-mental object that causes them. If this is right, "same idea" is, in Locke's mouth, multiply ambiguous, not only as between token and type, but between qualitative and significative sameness, sameness of idea *qua* sign.[33]

Locke requires sameness of idea for successful communication, but in which of these senses of "same?" Obviously it is impossible for two minds to have the same token of a given idea; this is what Frege insists upon time and again in "Thoughts." Sameness of type, then, is at issue. But within sameness of type, we can still ask whether Locke requires qualitative or significative sameness. Locke says that the hypothesis that an object produces in several minds qualitatively different ideas carries no "Imputation of *Falshood* to our simple *Ideas*" (II.xxxii.15: 389), and that someone in this state of affairs would be able to "distinguish Things for his Use by those

---

[32] Note that Locke does not think the problem meaningless or nonsensical, even though he acknowledges that there is in principle no way to ascertain the qualitative sameness of color ideas.

[33] Compare Sydney Shoemaker (1982, p. 365). Shoemaker distinguishes between qualitative and what he calls "intentional" sameness: "If Fred's house looked yellow to him at both t1 and t2, then with respect to color his house 'looked the same' to him at those two times in the sense that his experiences of it on those two occasions were *of* the same objective color, or had the same color as their 'intentional object.' Call this the 'intentional' sense of 'looks the same.'" Significative sameness differs from Shoemaker's intentional sameness only in that the former requires an idea of a color to be evidence for the existence of a physical object capable of causing that idea.

Appearances, and understand, and signify those distinctions, marked by the Names *Blue* and *Yellow*" (*ibid.*; see II.xxiii.8: 300). Thus all that is necessary for successful communication, at least where ideas of secondary qualities are involved, is significative sameness.

There is an arbitrariness to ideas of secondary qualities mirroring that of words. Unlike ideas of primary qualities, those of, say, color do not resemble their objects. Thus introspecting on their content tells us nothing about what they represent. Instead, we must look to their role as evidence of the qualities of the external objects fitted to produce them. Just as we might have made "dung" the sign of the idea of cake, God might have made the idea having the qualitative content *blue* the sign of an external object that in this possible world produces the quale *red*.

We can now turn our attention to the epistemic form of the question with which we began. To know that the word "blue" stands for the same idea for both of us would amount to knowing whether we were using "blue" to stand for the same idea *qua* sign. So if we have reasons to believe that our ideas causally co-vary, then, whatever their qualitative content, we can say they are the same. Such reasons lie outside Locke's purview, as they could only be supplied by empirical science; nevertheless, our common constitution provides some grounds for believing that there is this kind of causal co-variance among our ideas.[34] Moreover, the epistemic role of simple ideas will presumably show itself in the subject's inferences.

This puts us in a position to understand Frege's worries, for his main argument against "psychologism" turns on the identity conditions of propositions and thoughts of those propositions. In "Negation," Frege entertains the view that negation is separation, and affirmation, combination. As we have seen, this conforms to the outline of Locke's view, though some qualification is necessary to make clear that these acts are sub-propositional. Frege asks:

What then are these objects, which negation is supposed to separate? Not parts of sentences; equally, not parts of a thought. Things in the outside world? They do not bother about our negating. Mental images in the interior world of the person who negates? But then how does the juryman know which of his images he ought to separate in given circumstances? The question put before him does not indicate any to him. It may evoke images in him. But the images evoked in the jurymen's inner worlds are different; and in that case each juryman would perform his own act of separation in his own inner world, and this would not be a verdict.[35]

---

[34] Note that, since not all Lockean ideas are indicative signs, there are some ideas whose sameness might be qualitative rather than significative.

[35] Frege (1977, pp. 39–40).

The same kind of point is made in "Thoughts," except that here Frege brings out more clearly the subjectivist and solipsistic consequences he sees as following from the view that thoughts are simply private mental contents. Frege writes:

If every thought requires an owner and belongs to the contents of his consciousness, then the thought has this owner alone; and there is no science common to many on which many could work, but perhaps I have my science, a totality of thoughts whose owner I am, and another person has his. Each of us is concerned with the contents of his own consciousness. No contradiction between the two sciences would then be possible, and it would really be idle to dispute about truth; as idle, indeed almost as ludicrous, as for two people to dispute whether a hundred-mark note were genuine, when each meant the one he himself had in his pocket and understood the word "genuine" in his own particular sense. If someone takes thoughts to be ideas, what he then accepts as true is, on his own view, the contents of consciousness, and does not properly concern other people at all. If he heard from me the opinion that a thought is not an idea he could not dispute it, for, indeed, it would not now concern him.[36]

Frege's critique of the position that equates thoughts, the objects of judgment, with ideas, is sometimes strikingly close to Mill's famous objection to Locke. For instance, Frege offers this as a *reductio*: "if I state something about my brother, I do not state it about the idea that I have of my brother."[37] But to say that words signify ideas in no way entails that all of our talk is about our own ideas. As I argued in chapter one, it is open to Locke to accept that language, at least sometimes, is "about" or "refers to" public objects, so long as this is reducible to the signification relation, plus the intentionality of mental contents. That is, to say that the word "dog" in certain contexts refers to dogs is just to say that in general someone speaking the word provides us with evidence upon which we may infer that she is thinking of dogs. The work of "aboutness," if you like, is done at the mental, not the linguistic, level. This move allows Locke to parry Mill's objection.

Similarly, *pace* Frege, to say that we are immediately acquainted only with our own ideas does not entail that we cannot be aware of anything else:[38] ideas, for a representationalist like Locke, are instead the very means by which we obtain this awareness of the external world.

---

[36] Frege (1977, p. 15).   [37] Frege (1977, p. 23).

[38] See "Thoughts" in Frege (1977), where Frege mounts an attack on what seems to be representationalism. He writes: "[e]ither the thesis that only what is my idea can be the object of my awareness is false, or all my knowledge and perception is limited to my range of ideas . . . In this case I should have only an inner world and I should know nothing of other people" (1977, p. 19). One of the dangers of Frege's apparent reluctance in this essay to name those figures he takes to have held an opposing view is that the critique he offers has trouble finding a target. Certainly at least this portion of it does not tell against Locke.

But Frege goes beyond Mill in the two passages I have just quoted. The question is, under what conditions can we say that two people are having the same thought, or affirming (or denying) the same proposition? Frege argues that if the limits of our Cartesian theaters are the limits of our language, it will be impossible for us ever to disagree. Locke's response would be to point to his account of sameness of idea. Locke requires that the ideas be tokens of the same type, and that (at least in some cases, such as those of ideas of secondary qualities) they have what I have been calling significative, and not necessarily qualitative, sameness.[39]

But what about the act of the mind signified by a particle term? Here only type identity can reasonably be required. Your act of negating and mine cannot be numerically one; but nothing stops them from being instances of separation, and this is what matters, on Locke's view.

Frege, of course, will have none of this. He proclaims that "two men do not have the same sense impressions though they may have similar ones."[40] Whatever appearance this has of being an obvious truth is deceptive. Unless one assumes that numerical identity of ideas or sense impressions is the only kind worth having, the only kind relevant to the issues we have been exploring, this consideration goes no distance at all toward substantiating Frege's claim that his opponents are committed to what we might call linguistic solipsism.

What I have offered here does not, of course, amount to a complete vindication of Locke's view. I hope only to have shown that Locke's view cannot be dismissed as easily as many of his critics believe. In particular, the privacy of the mental does not preclude successful communication and indeed Lockean *ersatz* reference to public objects and qualities. The next chapter completes the evaluative portion of this work by assessing Locke's view in light of more contemporary developments in the philosophy of language.

---

[39] Ascertaining significative sameness, of course, requires moving beyond the Cartesian theater to make claims about such extra-mental events as causal relations between physical objects and our sense organs. This is another instance in which the metaphysical scheme Locke offers needs to be invoked in understanding his views about language. See chapter seven.

[40] Frege (1977, p. 26).

CHAPTER 7

Conclusion

Although something has been done above to situate Locke in a contemporary context, the reader may well wonder about the importance of all of this for the contemporary philosopher. What, when all is said and done, does Locke have to say to us?

By way of at once answering this question and drawing together the threads of this project as a whole, I shall step back for a moment from the details of Locke's view and ask whether an approach to language on Locke's lines is viable. As I indicated at the outset, I fully expect philosophers who have felt the twin influences of Frege and the Kripke/Putnam view of reference to be hostile to Locke's position. The claim that one's mental representations fix the reference of one's words is controversial enough; the additional claim that at bottom there is no such thing as reference is apt to sound paradoxical. It would be well to begin our assessment of Locke, then, by examining Putnam's arguments against the broadly Lockean position that meaning is a matter of mental representation.

Having argued that Locke's approach has the resources to answer these arguments and that mental representations can plausibly be said to mediate the word/world connection, I go on to assess the particular relations and mechanisms Locke thinks connect a (categorematic) word and a mental representation on one hand and such a representation and the world on the other. In so doing, we shall gain a clearer overview of Locke's philosophy as a whole.

WORD AND WORLD

Many contemporary philosophers of language would part ways with Locke right at the start. Any approach that posits the mental as a *tertium quid* is bound to have a decidedly backwards air about it. In particular, it is common to read that Hilary Putnam has shown (along with Kripke) that meanings "ain't in the head."

Details aside, Locke clearly holds a version of mentalism: the psychological state of the speaker determines the reference of his words. My claim that reference can be analyzed as a construction out of signification (see chapter one) does not affect the central point: one's ideas and mental acts determine what one "is talking about" in the pre-theoretical sense of this phrase. By contrast, Putnam argues that psychological states cannot fix reference because two beings might be in exactly the same psychological state and yet refer to different things. I shall show that Putnam's arguments do not support this conclusion. Lockean mentalism remains untouched.

Putnam's first argument deploys his famous Twin Earth example.[1] Suppose an Earthman, Oscar, and his Twin-Earth counterpart, call him Toscar, are atom-for-atom qualitatively identical. Putnam asks us to imagine that they have not only the same physical structure but the same thoughts and "interior monologue"; in short, they share all the same psychological states. It happens that on Twin Earth water is not H_2O but XYZ. What is the extension of "water" for Toscar? Since he is on Twin Earth, it must be XYZ. For Oscar, however, the extension is good old H_2O. So psychological states alone do not fix the extension of "water."

For this argument to have even the appearance of proving what it claims to prove, it must stipulate that Oscar and Toscar are in the same psychological state. This begs the question. The mentalist will argue precisely that they are *not* in fact in the same state.[2] The mentalist might suggest that psychological states themselves are individuated in part by their connections with the environment. Consider Locke's causal-cum-teleological account of mental representation. Since simple ideas represent the objects that (God has intended to) cause them, Oscar's idea of water and Toscar's idea of water *are not* the same ideas, even if they are qualitatively identical. Although Locke holds that psychological states fix reference (in the attenuated sense specified above), he does not think that psychological states themselves are individuated by their qualitative contents. Instead, it is their causal/teleological link to extra-mental objects that makes them states *of* a given thing or quality (if we abstract from Locke's distinct account of the workings of natural kind terms). Locke's mentalism supplemented by his causal theory of representation makes him immune to Twin Earth-style counterexamples.

---

[1] Putnam (1973, pp. 701–2).

[2] The dialectical moves in the Twin Earth debate are paralleled by those in arguments about the identity of indiscernibles. As Ian Hacking (1975b) has shown, the standard counterexamples (e.g., the alleged possibility of qualitatively identical spheres) to Leibniz's view invariably beg the question by assuming that there are *two* such spheres, or what have you.

Even if we grant that Oscar and Toscar are in the same mental state, however, Eddy Zemach has shown that Putnam's conclusion does not follow. According to Putnam, "water" in Earth English refers to water because it has the same nature as "most of the stuff I and others in my linguistic community have, on other occasions, called 'water.'"[3] But who constitutes Putnam's "linguistic community?" If it includes the Twin Earthians, then "water" does not refer to H_2O; either it is not a substance word at all (which seems absurd), or it refers to (H_2O v XYZ). (In fact, many of our substance words ("glue," "paper," even "water," which refers to both heavy water and H_2O) do have disjunctive extensions.) Putnam obviously does not want the Twin Earthians to be counted as members of the same linguistic community; but why? Where is the argument for excluding them? Note that Putnam cannot say that the Twin Earthians aren't part of the same linguistic community because they use water to refer to XYZ rather than H_2O; this is question-begging.

Putnam sometimes invokes Kripke's causal theory of reference in this connection. Consider Putnam's account of how "electricity" gets its meaning. For most of us, we "learn the word from someone linked by a chain of such transmissions to an introducing event."[4] An initial "dubbing" establishes the reference of the word; thereafter, the word continues to refer to the initially ostended or described kind, even if speakers come to have radically mistaken beliefs about that kind. Thus on both Earth and Twin Earth Putnam wishes us to suppose that an initial act of ostension or description allows Oscar, even if he did not himself perform this initial act, to refer to H_2O, and Toscar to XYZ. Their relationship to these different initial dubbings put Oscar and Toscar in distinct linguistic communities.

Zemach points out that it is now epistemically possible that "water" refers to pig urine. For we can never hope to know the circumstances surrounding the initial introduction of a word. Even if there was such a mythical act of naming in the distant past, it is impossible for us ever to learn anything about that act. Zemach concludes: "any theory which has as a result that we do not and cannot know what is the correct reference of the word 'water,' or any other substance term, cannot be right."[5]

Putnam links the Kripke view with his second main argument, the argument from the division of linguistic labor (DLL). On the causal view, our words refer as they do because we are members of a linguistic community that stands in the proper causal chain leading back to the original dubbing of the natural kind. We should stop thinking of language as "private

[3] Putnam (1973, p. 702), quoted in Zemach (1976, p. 118).
[4] Putnam (1975, p. 202).   [5] Zemach (1976, p. 123).

property."[6] In some cases, it is in part our relation to the rest of the community that explains our ability to refer. For example, it is not necessary that everyone using the word "gold" properly has the ability to tell real gold from iron pyrite. Some of us rely on a special subset of speakers who *do* have this ability; our use of "gold" "depends upon a structured cooperation between [us] and the speakers in the relevant subsets."[7] In many cases, we are willing to defer to experts on the extension of our sortal terms. All of this seems true. But it does not support Putnam's overall claim.

To see why, note that Putnam grants that some words, such as "chair," do not exhibit DLL; others did not at one time but now do. How are we to determine which is the case?[8] Consider Oscar once again. Oscar cannot tell beeches from elms; walking through the woods, he will apply "elm" indiscriminately. Does "elm" in Oscar's idiolect exemplify DLL? We can't decide this question by deferring to the scientists. Nor can we assume that the answer must be "yes." Oscar might well use the term to refer to all trees that have some feature or set of features in common and not give a hoot what the experts will say. Unlike Putnam, Locke *can* answer this question: we must ask Oscar about his concept of elm and see whether he intends "elm" to signify "whatever the experts mean by 'elm'" or not. DLL is thus perfectly consistent with Lockean mentalism. In fact, as Zemach argues, it seems to *presuppose* either mentalism or some other "traditional" account. For Putnam himself cannot simply stipulate that "elm" in Oscar's idiolect exemplifies DLL. Whether it does or not, according to Locke, will turn on the content of Oscar's psychological states (and their extra-mental causes).

Locke's position, then, does not fall to these arguments against mentalism. For all that, we must not overestimate the gap between Locke's position and the Putnam/Kripke view. As I have suggested above, Locke conceives of mental representation at least partly in terms of causal connection. It is not much of an exaggeration to say that Locke's view is what results if we alter Putnam's so that the mental, as opposed to the linguistic, is the source of intentionality. As we shall see (chapter seven), Locke's insistence on the causal connections between mental representations and their referents is not so far removed after all from Putnam-style externalism.

WORD AND MIND

I have argued that it is reasonable to hold a Lockean view of language in the face of Putnam-style arguments against mentalism. This is far from a

---

[6] Putnam (1975, p. 203).   [7] Putnam (1975, p. 228).
[8] Zemach (1976, p. 125) offers a version of this argument.

defense of Locke's view, of course, since mentalism can take many different forms. The claim that the word–world connection is mediated by the mind says nothing about either the word–mind or mind–world connection. A fuller assessment of Locke's view must therefore consider his proposed accounts of those two relations. In this section, I shall offer some remarks on the first of these.

I have already granted that, as a full account of language, Locke's position is woefully inadequate. Locke simply has nothing to say on the multifarious uses of language; topics such as illocutionary acts are never addressed and pretty clearly cannot be made to fit the Procrustean bed of signification. To take this as a devastating critique, however, is to miss Locke's point in engaging in his inquiry in the first place. He is after an account of the regions of language that are of central importance to his epistemology and metaphysics.

If we then implicitly limit the application of Locke's view to what we might call "descriptive" or "fact-stating" uses of language, it becomes much more plausible. True, it would be implausible, phenomenologically, to say that we always take others' words as indications of their mental acts and objects. But as we have seen, Locke grants that in practice most of us do not consciously infer a speaker's thoughts from her words, but simply have an idea "raised up" in us. That this sometimes causes confusion hardly needs saying; that it often takes place also seems clear.

Much of the apparent implausibility of the linguistic thesis disappears once one sees that Locke in no way claims that language is *about* our ideas. As we have seen, intentionality, for Locke, takes place at the mental, not linguistic, level. In this sense of "aboutness," words are not about *anything*. Instead, they are signals others can (although they often do not) use to infer what is going on in our minds. The Fregean notions of *Sinn* and *Bedeutung* have no real place in Locke's theory, although I have argued that Locke can reconstruct the apparent facts of reference through a slightly cumbersome, but perfectly plausible, reductive analysis.

Locke's view is built around the claim that the linguistic inherits its intentionality from the mental.[9] This view of intentionality strikes me as right. There are of course many other positions besides that of Putnam that challenge the role of mental representations in fixing meaning. Indeed, some philosophers, such as Paul Churchland, treat talk of mental representations as part of a defective "folk psychology" that will one day be supplanted by

---

[9] Perhaps the most famous argument for the claim that the intentionality of language is primary to that of the mental is offered by Sellars (1963).

a complete neuroscience. This position has come under withering attack.[10] Nor do I see much hope for other eliminativist strategies, such as that of Daniel Dennett. Dennett's instrumentalism about intentionality strikes me as neither plausible nor internally coherent.[11] There is not space here to mount a full attack on these competing views. It must be enough here to note that the core of Locke's position has emerged unscathed from the objections we have considered.

MIND AND WORLD

Even if we grant Locke this much, the crucial connection between mind and world has yet to be drawn. The first group of problems we must examine center on Locke's "ideism," in Sergeant's phrase. If all knowledge is propositional (II.xxxiii.19: 401), and all (mental) propositions are made by affirming or denying one idea of another, how can we be said to know anything outside our own minds? In particular, how can Locke account for our ability to predicate real existence of the objects of the senses? The second problem I shall discuss concerns Locke's account of representation. As we have seen, Locke offers a causal-cum-teleological view of representation, intended to establish the link between mind and world. We saw above (chapter one) that the teleological element of his view allows him to answer the two most formidable objections to causal theories. But what can Locke say to the skeptic, who argues that, having placed us behind a "veil of ideas," Locke has in effect severed any possible epistemic link between mind and world?

Let us begin with knowledge. If propositions consist of affirmations and denials of one idea of another, in what sense can we say that knowledge is *about* real things, and not just ideas? We have already seen a general answer to this question in discussing Locke's view of representation: the ideas themselves (in some cases) represent real things. But it is obscure how this ideational account can ever make sense of knowledge of real existence. For to say that *x* exists would seem to be to go beyond the bounds of one's own ideas.

As A.D. Woozley puts it,

On the accepted interpretation of Locke's theory of ideas, his account of knowledge runs immediately into an insuperable objection. Given that knowledge is what he defines it to be, the perception of the agreement or disagreement of ideas, the

---

[10] See Crane (1995).
[11] For a thorough critique of Dennett's "intentional stance," see Lynne Rudder Baker (1989).

only propositions that even in principle could be known would be hypothetical non-existential propositions, e.g. those of mathematics. Existential propositions not only could not in fact be verified (for that would require breaking out of the circle of ideas), but they could not even in principle be candidates for knowledge, because such propositions not only do not assert a relation between one idea and others, but are not relational propositions at all.[12]

Woozley lays the blame for this "insuperable difficulty" at the door of representationalist readings of Locke. I have argued briefly for such a reading above. But if we look more carefully at Locke's conception of experience, we shall see that the difficulty Woozley raises is indeed superable.

In fact, Woozley's objection stems in part from the same misunderstanding of Locke's view of language I have been fighting against throughout this work. A proposition does not necessarily *assert* that the ideas in question agree or disagree, even though this is what makes them true or false. A mental proposition is *about* the things the ideas refer to. This, however, is only the beginning of the story. For in order to have *real* knowledge, one's ideas must reach out beyond themselves to extra-mental things and their qualities.

In IV.iv, Locke writes,

I Doubt not but my Reader, by this time, may be apt to think, that I have been all this while only building a Castle in the Air; and be ready to say to me, To what purpose all this stir? Knowledge, say you, is only the perception of the agreement or disagreement of our own *Ideas*: but who knows what those *Ideas* may be? . . . 'Tis no matter how Things are: so a Man observe but the agreement of his own Imaginations, and talk conformably, it is all Truth, all Certainty . . . But *of what use is all this* fine *Knowledge of Men's own Imaginations*, to a Man that enquires after the reality of Things? (IV.iv.1: 562–3)

Knowledge *per se* is propositional for Locke, since it is the perception of the agreement or disagreement of ideas; a bit of knowledge can be said to be *real* just in case the ideas involved in the true mental proposition conform to or agree with "the reality of Things" (IV.iv.3: 563). This means that we must distinguish between what makes a proposition true from what makes a true proposition count as *real* knowledge. The former is simply the agreement or disagreement of its constituent ideas (depending upon whether the proposition is an affirmation or denial); the latter is the relation between each constituent idea and its extra-mental object.

---

[12] Woozley (1964, p. 48). A century earlier T.H. Green had made the same point: Locke's subsumption of real existence under the agreement and disagreement of ideas "departs at once and openly from his definition, making it an agreement, not of idea with idea, but of an idea with 'actual real existence' " (quoted in Mattern 1998, p. 227).

(If either idea lacks such an object, the proposition is not a proper object of real knowledge.) The distinction between real knowledge and knowledge that involves ideas that lack referents (such as "an Harpy is not a Centaur" (IV.iv.1: 563)) turns not on the agreement or disagreement of ideas but on whether the individual ideas involved conform to extra-mental objects. Although Locke's criterion for knowledge seems clearly internalist, insofar as the contents of ideas are immediately present to the mind, his criterion for real knowledge is not. That is, on my reading of Locke, it is perfectly possible for someone to meet the criterion for real knowledge and not know it. Ideally, of course, we want not only to have real knowledge but to know that our knowledge is indeed real. Under what circumstances can we be justified in believing that the criterion for real knowledge has been met?[13]

Locke's answer invokes, in the first place, his view of representation. Given his account of simple ideas of sensation, he can claim that they conform to things because they are the effects of real objects operating on our senses; moreover, this causal connection was instituted by God to allow us to deal effectively with our environment. In IV.iv, however, Locke offers further reasons for thinking that simple ideas provide real knowledge.

The first [sort of ideas that we can know agree with things] are simple *Ideas*, which since the Mind, as has been shewed, can by no means make it self, must necessarily be the product of Things operating on the Mind in a natural way, and producing therein those Perceptions which by the Wisdom and Will of our Maker they are ordained and adapted to. (IV.iv.4: 563–4)

One detects more than a whiff in such passages of Descartes's anti-skeptical strategy: the benevolence of the Deity assures us that our sensory faculties reliably indicate the presence of real, extra-mental objects. Locke's passage also suggests the more familiar claim that since the ideas of sensation cannot be caused by the mind itself, they must be caused by objects in an external world. Both strategies are subject to grave (and rather obvious) difficulties I shall not go into.

But Locke need not have even flirted with such strategies. For on his view, the representational content of an idea is fixed by its cause (and ultimately by God's intentions in setting up the causal connections), and so there is no sense to be made of the proposal that simple ideas might fail to represent their intended objects under normal conditions (see chapter one). As a reply to the Cartesian skeptic, this line of thought is totally

---

[13] I am focusing here on the reality of knowledge involving our simple ideas of sensation. Locke offers different accounts of the reality of knowledge where moral, mathematical, and other forms of knowledge are concerned. See IV.iv: 564–70.

unpersuasive: Locke's move, from that point of view, would only push that problem back, since now the introspectible content of an idea is no longer a guide to what it represents. (Compare the common reaction to Putnam's response to the brain-in-a-vat scenario: if Putnam were right, that would make Vatman all the worse off, since now he no longer knows even what his own words mean!) But it is a central feature of externalism about mental representation that it does *not* proceed from the first-person point of view. It is just not clear why we should feel compelled to attempt the Cartesian project of reconstructing the world on the basis of the contents of our own minds. Locke's externalism about representation, I submit, makes him similarly hostile to the position that philosophy must proceed from the first-person perspective. This is borne out in his flippant attitude toward skepticism, evident throughout IV.iv. The core of his response, that our simple ideas represent their causes, is clearly question-begging from the skeptic's point of view; but Locke is unconcerned because he refuses to occupy that perspective when discussing questions of knowledge.[14]

Nevertheless, the details of Locke's view on existence make his position difficult to defend. In a mental proposition asserting existence, one affirms the idea of existence of another idea. The idea of existence itself is intromit-ted by the senses, on Locke's view: it is "suggested by to the Understanding, by every Object without, and every *Idea* within" (I.vii.7: 131). Our experi-ence of the whiteness of the paper before our eyes carries with it the idea existence, and so justifies (and allows us to create) the propositional claim that the paper exists. Thus existence is as it were bundled with all our sensory experiences.

Whether the details of Locke's account are defensible will turn, in part, on whether he has the right conception of existence, as Woozley clearly sees. Locke treats existence as a predicate, and claims of existence on a par with ordinary predications. From Suárez to Kant, this treatment has been challenged. But perhaps the most articulate foe of Locke's position here is Hume.

As is well known, Hume argues that belief is nothing more than "a particular manner of forming an idea: And as the same idea can only be vary'd by a variation of its degrees of force and vivacity; it follows upon the whole, that belief is a lively idea produc'd by a relation to a present impression . . ."[15] What is less well known is how Hume arrives at this somewhat idiosyncratic view. In fact, he begins his argument by focusing on the central case of existence:

---

[14] See Ayers (1991, vol. 1, p. 38). Ayers neglects the teleological component of Locke's view.
[15] Hume (1978, p. 97).

'Tis . . . evident, that the idea of existence is nothing different from the idea of any object, and that when after the simple conception of any thing we wou'd conceive it as existent, we in reality make no addition to or alteration on our first idea. Thus when we affirm, that God is existent, we simply form the idea of such a being, as he is represented to us; nor is the existence, which we attribute to him, conceiv'd by a particular idea, which we join to the idea of his other qualities, and can again separate and distinguish from them . . . I likewise maintain, that the belief of the existence joins no new ideas to those, which compose the idea of the object. When I think of God, when I think of him as existent, and when I believe him to be existent, my idea of him neither encreases nor diminishes.[16]

Hume is hostile throughout the *Treatise* toward views such as Locke's that treat propositions as composed of distinct ideas combined by a mental act.[17] David Owen has shown that this hostility has its source in Hume's objection to the way in which such views must treat affirmations of existence.[18] A subject/predicate treatment of such affirmations clearly requires that we have a separate idea of existence, distinct from that of the object itself. *Every* idea and impression, according to Hume, is conceived as existent; either this conception is nothing other than the force or vivacity of the idea, or it is itself a distinct idea that accompanies every other perception. The latter option is unavailable within Hume's system, for it is one of his fundamental principles that no two ideas are inseparable.[19]

Whatever we make of Hume's own position, he is on firm ground in asserting that existence is not a predicate. His own account is vulnerable to a number of objections, chief among them, that he has no way to account for propositional content.[20] A plausible treatment of existence, it seems, had to await the development of quantificational logic.

Locke's view of the representative powers of simple ideas allows him to link mind and world in a very plausible way and to sidestep skepticism. His implicit opposition to externalist views of linguistic meaning, such as Putnam's, does not prevent him from adopting an externalist stance with regard to mental representation in the case of simple ideas. The arbitrariness of language is not mirrored at the level of mental representation.

Locke has not enclosed us in a "circle of ideas" from which knowledge of existence would require us to break out; instead, ideas are precisely the means we have of knowing the external world. This point is often missed because it is so obviously question-begging in the face of Cartesian skepticism. But, as I have suggested, perhaps there are some questions we should be content to beg.

---

[16] Hume (1978, p. 94).   [17] See esp. his footnote at (1978, p. 96).
[18] See Owen (forthcoming).   [19] This is the dilemma Hume poses; see his (1978, p. 66).
[20] See Owen (forthcoming).

The goal of this study was to clarify Locke's conception of signification and use it to illuminate core areas of his epistemology and metaphysics. Once Locke's conception of signification is rightly understood, much else about his view that is otherwise puzzling falls into place. We have seen how Locke's position on syncategoremata and the nature of the proposition become intelligible, if not fully defensible, in this light. And his conception of the operations of the mind involved in human understanding gains much from his treatment of particles. In these respects, then, Locke's inquiries into the nature of language fit nicely with his announced "Historical, plain Method" (I.i.2: 44). Locke's descriptive project, directed as it is at the workings of the mind itself, would hardly be complete without these elements.

What is perhaps more important for our understanding of the early modern period, the sense in which Locke intends his conception of language to tell against competing views, especially those of the Aristotelians, becomes clear. His views have a normative, as well as a descriptive, side that allows him to deploy linguistic arguments. In particular, he argues that Aristotelian essentialism arises from a persistent and natural misunderstanding of the ways words function, given the purposes for which we use them. In this light, Locke's philosophy of language can be seen as part of an "error theory" about essentialism: it serves not only to expose fundamental errors but to explain their continuing appeal.

Whether one finds essentialism independently attractive will affect, if not determine, one's estimation of Locke's philosophy of language. Attacks on Aristotelianism were far from uncommon, of course, among Locke's predecessors. But Locke, arguably, does the most thorough job of attacking the Aristotelian form of essentialism. It took centuries before essentialism could be resurrected, the dust of the empiricist attacks brushed off, and made to look respectable once again, by the likes of Kripke and Marcus. Was Locke, then, just another modern empiricist who helped to throw philosophy off the scent? So Michael Ayers seems to believe; on his view, essentialism is at once common-sensical and philosophically correct. The Aristotelians largely had it right; Locke is the reason why philosophers fell "away from the truth."[21]

This is not the place to argue for the merits of nominalism or essentialism. But we can ask why essentialism seems so appealing in the first place. In my view, the chief attraction of essentialism is the work it can do in the key areas of causation and laws of nature. As we have seen, however, Locke's restricted nominalism does just as good a job of grounding laws of nature (and by

---

[21] Ayers (1981, p. 248).

extension, causality) as essentialism. For Locke can reconstruct laws of nature in terms of the particularized properties of the substances concerned (see chapter three). This is entirely independent of the question of natural kinds and essences. Indeed, I see it as one of Locke's chief achievements that he was able to distinguish the question of properties from that of natural kinds and essences, and to offer distinct treatments of each. We can be skeptical of natural kinds and yet endorse (particularized) properties as key ingredients in the best account of the laws of nature and causation. Locke provides a very reasonable way of acknowledging the human contribution to our pre-theoretical ways of carving up reality while still respecting the limits reality imposes on our conceptual activity.

Bibliography

Aaron, R.I. 1952. *The Theory of Universals*. Oxford: Clarendon Press.

Aarsleff, Hans. 1964. "Leibniz on Locke on Language." *American Philosophical Quarterly* 1: 165–88.

Alston, William. 1964. *The Philosophy of Language*. Englewood Cliffs, NJ: Prentice Hall.

Aquinas, St. Thomas. 1945. *Basic Writings*. 2 vols. Edited by Anton Pegis. New York: Random House.

———. 1970. *Commentary on the Posterior Analytics*. Translated by F.R. Larcher. New York: Magi Books.

———. 1993. *Selected Philosophical Writings*. Edited by T. McDermott. Oxford: Oxford University Press.

Aristotle. 1984. *The Complete Works of Aristotle*. 2 vols. Edited by Jonathan Barnes. Princeton, NJ: Princeton University Press.

———. 1989. *Prior Analytics*. Translated by Robin Smith. Indianapolis: Hackett.

Armstrong, D.M. 1978. *Universals and Scientific Realism*. 2 vols. Cambridge: Cambridge University Press.

———. 1989. *Universals: An Opinionated Introduction*. Boulder, CO: Westview Press, 1989.

———. 1991. "Arda Denkel's Resemblance Nominalism." *Philosophical Quarterly* 41: 478–82.

Arnauld, Antoine. 1775. *Oeuvres de Messire Antoine Arnauld*. 43 vols. Paris: Sigismond D'Arnay.

———. 1990. *On True and False Ideas*. Translated by Stephen Gaukroger. Manchester: Manchester University Press.

Arnauld, Antoine and Claude Lancelot. 1966. *Grammaire générale et raisonnée, ou La Grammaire de Port-Royal*. Edited by Herbert E. Brekle. Stuttgart: Friedrich Fromman Verlag.

———. 1975. *The Port-Royal Grammar*. Translated and edited by Jacques Rieux and Bernard E. Rollin. Paris: Mouton.

Arnauld, Antoine and Pierre Nicole. 1964. *The Art of Thinking*. Translated by James Dickoff and Patricia James. New York: Bobbs-Merrill.

———. 1970. *La Logique, ou L'art de Penser*. Paris: Flammarion.

————. 1996. *Logic or the Art of Thinking*. Translated and edited by Jill Vance Buroker. Cambridge: Cambridge University Press.

Ashworth, E.J. 1981. "Do Words Signify Ideas or Things?" *Journal of the History of Philosophy* 19: 299–326.

————. 1984. "Locke on Language." *Canadian Journal of Philosophy* 14: 45–73.

————. 1988. "The Historical Origins of John Poinsot's *Treatise on Signs*." *Semiotica* 69: 129–47.

————. 1990. "Domingo de Soto and the Doctrine of Signs." In *De Ortu Grammaticae*, edited by G.L. Bursill-Hall, Sten Ebbesen, and Konrad Koerner. Philadelphia: John Benjamins.

Augustine. 1958. *On Christian Doctrine*. Translated by D.W. Robertson. New York: Bobbs-Merrill.

————. 1975. *De Dialectica*. Translated by B. Darrell Jackson. Boston: D. Reidel.

————. 1991. *The Trinity*. Translated by Edmund Hill. New York: New City Press, 1991.

————. 1995. *Against the Academicians and The Teacher*. Translated by Peter King. Indianapolis: Hackett.

Ayer, A.J. 1946. *Language, Truth and Logic*. New York: Dover.

Ayers, M.R. 1975. "Introduction." In *George Berkeley: Philosophical Works, Including the Works on Vision*, edited by M.R. Ayers. London: J.M. Dent.

————. 1981. "Locke Versus Aristotle on Natural Kinds." *Journal of Philosophy* 78: 247–72.

————. 1986. "Are Locke's 'Ideas' Images, Intentional Objects, or Natural Signs?" *The Locke Newsletter* 17: 3–36.

————. 1991. *Locke: Epistemology and Ontology*. London: Routledge.

————. 1997. "Review of the *Cambridge Companion to Locke*." *The Locke Newsletter* 28: 157–89.

————. 1998a. "The Foundations of Knowledge and the Logic of Substance: the Structure of Locke's General Philosophy." In *Locke*, edited by Vere Chappell. Oxford: Oxford University Press.

————. 1998b. "Ideas and Objective Being." In *The Cambridge History of Seventeenth Century Philosophy*, edited by M.R. Ayers and Daniel Garber. 2 vols. Cambridge: Cambridge University Press.

Baker, Lynne Rudder. 1989. "Instrumental Intentionality." *Philosophy of Science* 56, 2: 303–16.

Behan, David. 2000. "Descartes and Formal Signs." In *Descartes' Natural Philosophy*, edited by Stephen Gaukroger, John Schuster, and John Sutton. London: Routledge.

Bennett, Jonathan. 1971. *Locke, Berkeley, Hume: Central Themes*. Oxford: Clarendon Press.

Berkeley, George. 1949–58. *The Works of George Berkeley*. 8 vols. Edited by A.A. Luce and T.E. Jessop. London: Thomas Nelson.

————. 1987. *Berkeley's Manuscript Introduction*. Edited by Bertil Belfrage. Oxford: Doxa.

Blackburn, Simon. 1984. *Spreading the Word*. Oxford: Oxford University Press.

Bolton, Martha. 1998a. "The Relevance of Locke's Theory of Ideas to his Doctrine of Nominal Essence and Anti-essentialist Semantic Theory." In *Locke*, edited by Vere Chappell. Oxford: Oxford University Press.

————. 1998b. "Universals, Essences, and Abstract Entities." In *The Cambridge History of Seventeenth Century Philosophy*, edited by M.R. Ayers and Daniel Garber. 2 vols. Cambridge: Cambridge University Press.

Burnyeat, Myles F. 1982. "The Origins of Non-Deductive Inference." In *Science and Speculation: Studies in Hellenistic Theory and Practice*, edited by Jonathan Barnes, Jacques Brunschwig, Myles Burnyeat, and Malcolm Schofield. Cambridge: Cambridge University Press.

Buroker, Jill Vance. 1993. "The Port-Royal Semantics of Terms." *Synthese* 96, 3: 455–76.

Cajetan (Cardinal Thomas de Vio). 1953. *The Analogy of Names*. Translated by E.A. Bushinski. Pittsburgh: Pittsburgh University Press.

Coimbran Commentators. 1976. *Commentarii Conimbricenses in dialecticam Aristotelis* (1607). Reprinted by Hildesheim: G. Olms.

Crane, Tim. 1995. *The Mechanical Mind*. London: Penguin.

Cummins, Robert. 1989. *Meaning and Mental Representation*. Cambridge, MA: Harvard University Press.

Denkel, Arda. 1989. "Real Resemblances." *Philosophical Quarterly* 39: 36–56.

Descartes, René. 1984. *The Philosophical Writings of Descartes*. Vols. 1 and 2, edited by John Cottingham, Robert Stoothoff, and Dugald Murdoch; vol. 3, edited by Cottingham, Stoothoff, Murdoch, and Anthony Kenny. New York: Cambridge University Press.

Digby, Sir Kenelm. 1657. *Two Treatises: in the one of which, the nature of bodies, in the other the nature of mans soule is looked into: in way of discovery of the immortality of reasonable soules*. London.

Donagan, Alan. 1971. "Universals and Metaphysical Realism." In *The Problem of Universals*, edited by C. Landesman. New York: Basic Books.

Doney, Willis. 1956. "Locke's Abstract Ideas." *Philosophy and Phenomenological Research* 16, 3: 406–9.

Doyle, John P. 1984. "The *Conimbricenses* on the Relations Involved in Signs." In *Semiotica*, edited by John Deeley. New York: University Press.

Dretske, Fred. 1990. "Misrepresentation." In *Mind and Cognition*, edited by William G. Lycan. Oxford: Blackwell.

Evans, Gareth. 1982. *The Varieties of Reference*. Oxford: Clarendon Press.

Ferguson, Sally. 2001. "Lockian Teleosemantics." *Locke Studies* 1: 105–22.

Flew, Antony. 1993. "Was Berkeley a Precursor of Wittgenstein?" In *Alciphron: In Focus*, edited by David Berman. London: Routledge.

Fodor, Jerry. 1984. "Semantics, Wisconsin Style." *Synthese* 59: 231–50.

————. 1987. *Psychosemantics*. Cambridge, MA: MIT Press.

Frege, Gottlob. 1950. *The Foundations of Arithmetic*. Translated by J.L. Austin. Evanston: Northwestern University Press.

_____. 1959. *Collected Papers on Mathematics, Logic, and Philosophy.* Translated by Max Black. Oxford: Blackwell.

_____. 1977. *Logical Investigations.* Translated by P.T. Geach and R. H. Stoothoff. New Haven: Yale University Press.

_____. 1980. *Translations From the Philosophical Writings of Gottlob Frege.* Edited by Peter Geach and Max Black. 3rd edn. Oxford: Blackwell.

_____. 1997. *The Frege Reader.* Edited by Michael Beaney. London: Blackwell.

Gassendi, Pierre. 1972. *The Selected Works of Pierre Gassendi.* Edited by Craig Brush. New York: Johnson.

Geach, Peter. 1957. *Mental Acts.* London: Routledge and Kegan Paul.

_____. 1961. "Frege." In Geach and G.E.M. Anscombe, *Three Philosophers.* London: Blackwell.

_____. 1980. *Reference and Generality.* Ithaca: Cornell University Press.

Gilson, Etienne. 1956. *The Christian Philosophy of Thomas St. Aquinas.* Notre Dame: University of Notre Dame Press.

Grice, H.P. 1957. "Meaning." *Philosophical Review* 66: 377–88.

Guyer, Paul. 1994. "Locke's Philosophy of Language." In *The Cambridge Companion to Locke,* edited by Vere Chappell. Cambridge: Cambridge University Press.

Hacking, Ian. 1975a. "The Identity of Indiscernibles." *Journal of Philosophy* 72: 249–56.

_____. 1975b. *Why Does Language Matter to Philosophy?* Cambridge: Cambridge University Press.

Hanna, Robert. 1991. "How Ideas Became Meanings: Locke and the Foundations of Semantic Theory." *Review of Metaphysics*: 44: 775–805.

Harrison, John and Peter Laslett. 1971. *The Library of John Locke.* 2nd edition. Oxford: Clarendon Press.

Hobbes, Thomas. 1839–45. *The English Works of Thomas Hobbes.* 11 vols. Edited by William Molesworth. London: Richards.

_____. 1994. *Human Nature and De Corpore.* Oxford: Oxford University Press.

Hume, David. 1978. *A Treatise of Human Nature.* Edited by L.A. Selby-Bigge, revised by P.H. Nidditch. Oxford: Clarendon.

Hylton, Peter. 1984. "The Nature of the Proposition and the Revolt Against Idealism." In *Philosophy in History,* edited by Richard Rorty, J.B. Schneewind, and Quentin Skinner. Cambridge: Cambridge University Press.

_____. 1992. *Russell, Idealism, and the Emergence of Analytic Philosophy.* Oxford: Oxford University Press.

Inwood, Brad and L.P. Gerson. 1988. *Hellenistic Philosophy: Introductory Readings.* Indianapolis: Hackett.

Kant, Immanuel. 1958. *Critique of Pure Reason.* Translated by N.K. Smith. London: Macmillan.

_____. 1974. *Logic.* Translated by Robert Hartmann and Wolfgang Schwartz. New York: Dover, 1974.

Kenny, Anthony. 1994. *Frege.* London: Penguin.

Kretzmann, Norman. 1975. "The Main Thesis of Locke's Semantic Theory." In *Locke on Human Understanding*, edited by I.C. Tipton. Oxford: Oxford University Press. *Philosophical Review* 77. First published in (1968): 175–96.

Land, Stephen K. 1986. *The Philosophy of Language in Britain*. New York: AMS Press.

Landesman, Charles. 1976. "Locke's Theory of Meaning." *Journal of the History of Philosophy* 14: 23–35.

Lee, Henry. 1702. *Anti-skepticism: or notes upon each chapter of Mr. Locke's Essay*.

Leibniz, G.W. 1996. *New Essays on Human Understanding*. Translated and edited by Jonathan Bennett and Peter Remnant. Cambridge: Cambridge University Press.

Levin, Michael E. 1971. "Length Relativity." *Journal of Philosophy* 68, 6: 164–74.

Locke, John. 1812. *The Works of John Locke*. 11th edn. 10 vols. London: Otridge et al.

———. 1975. *An Essay concerning Human Understanding*. Edited by P.H. Nidditch. Oxford: Clarendon.

Long, A.A. and D.N. Sedley. 1987. *The Hellenistic Philosophers*. 2 vols. New York: Cambridge University Press.

Losonsky, Michael. 1994. "Locke on Meaning and Signification." In *Locke's Philosophy: Content and Context*, edited by G.A.J. Rogers. Oxford: Clarendon Press.

Loux, Michael. 1978. *Substance and Attribute*. Dordrecht: Reidel.

Lovejoy, Arthur O. 1907. "Kant's Classification of the Forms of Judgment." *Philosophical Review* 16: 588–603.

Lowe, E.J. 1995. *Locke on Human Understanding*. London: Routledge.

———. 2000. "Locke, Martin, and Substance." *Philosophical Quarterly* 50: 499–514.

MacDonald, Scott. 1993. "Theory of Knowledge." In *The Cambridge Companion to Aquinas*, edited by N. Kretzmann and E. Stump. Cambridge: Cambridge University Press.

MacIntyre, Alasdair. 1999. *Dependent Rational Animals*. Chicago: Open Court.

Mackie, J.L. 1974. "Locke's Anticipation of Kripke." *Analysis* 34: 177–80.

———. 1976. *Problems from Locke*. Oxford: Oxford University Press.

Markus, R.A. 1957. "St. Augustine on Signs." *Phronesis* 2: 60–83.

Martin, C.B. 1980. "Substance Substantiated." *Australasian Journal of Philosophy* 58, 1: 3–10.

Mattern, Ruth. 1998. "Locke: 'Our Knowledge, which All Consists in Propositions.'" In *Locke*, edited by Vere Chappell. Oxford: Oxford University Press.

Mattey, G.J. 1986. "Kant's Theory of Propositional Attitudes." *Kant-Studien* 77, 4: 423–40.

Matthews, H.E. 1971. "Locke, Malebranche, and the Representative Theory." *The Locke Newsletter* 2: 12–21.

McCann, Edwin. 1994. "Locke's Philosophy of Body." In *The Cambridge Companion to Locke*, edited by Vere Chappell. Cambridge: Cambridge University Press.

McCracken, Charles J. 1983. *Malebranche and British Philosophy*. Oxford: Clarendon Press.

Mill, J.S. 1867. *A System of Logic*. New York: Harper.

Nuchelmans, Gabriel. 1980. *Late Scholastic and Humanist Theories of the Proposition*. New York: North Holland.

———. 1983. *Judgment and Proposition from Descartes to Kant*. New York: North Holland.

———. 1986. "The Historical Background to Locke's Account of Particles." *Logique et Analyse* 29: 53–71.

Ott, W. 1997. "Locke and the Scholastics on Theological Discourse." *The Locke Newsletter* 28: 51–66.

———. 1999. "Locke and the Idea of God: A Reply to Vivienne Brown." *The Locke Newsletter* 30: 67–71.

———. 2002a. "Locke's Argument from Signification." *Locke Studies* 2: 145–76.

———. 2002b. "Propositional Attitudes in Modern Philosophy." *Dialogue* 41: 1–18.

———. 2002c. "Locke and Signification." *Journal of Philosophical Research* 27: 449–73.

Owen, David. "Locke and Hume on Belief, Judgment, and Assent." Forthcoming, *Topoi*.

Panza, Christopher. "Partial Consideration, Mental Separation, and General Reference." Forthcoming.

Philodemus. 1941. *De Signis*. Translated by W. and D. De Lacey. Philadelphia: American Philological Association.

Poinsot, John (John of St. Thomas). 1995. *Tractatus de Signis*. Translated and edited by John Deely. Berkeley: University of California Press.

Putnam, Hilary. 1973. "Meaning and Reference." *Journal of Philosophy* 70, 19: 699–711.

———. 1975. *Mind, Language, and Reality: Philosophical Papers, Vol. 2*. New York: Cambridge University Press.

Quine, Willard Van Orman. 1969. *Ontological Relativity and Other Essays*. New York: Columbia University Press.

Quintilian. 1920. *Institutio Oratoria*. Translated by H.E. Butler. 4 vols. Cambridge, MA: Harvard University Press.

Robinson, Richard. 1950. *Definition*. Oxford: Clarendon Press.

Russell, Bertrand. 1912. *The Problems of Philosophy*. Oxford: Oxford University Press.

———. 1937a. *The Philosophy of Leibniz*. London: Allen and Unwin.

———. 1937b. *Principles of Mathematics*. London: Allen and Unwin.

———. 1948. *Human Knowledge: Its Scope and Limits*. New York: Simon and Schuster.

———. 1983. *The Collected Papers of Bertrand Russell*. 8 vols. Edited by Elisabeth Eames and Kenneth Blackwell. London: Allen and Unwin.

———. 1992. *Logic and Knowledge*. London: Routledge.

Searle, John. 1987. "Indeterminacy, Empiricism, and the First Person." *Journal of Philosophy* 84, 3: 123–46.

Sedley, David. 1982. "On Signs." In *Science and Speculation: Studies in Hellenistic Theory and Practice*, edited by Jonathan Barnes, Jacques Brunschwig, Myles Burnyeat, and Malcolm Schofield. Cambridge: Cambridge University Press.

Sellars, Wilfrid. 1963. "Empiricism and the Philosophy of Mind." In *Science, Perception, and Reality*. Atascadero, CA: Ridgeview Publishing Company.

Sergeant, John. 1984. *Solid Philosophy Asserted Against the Fancies of the Ideists*. New York: Garland.

Shoemaker, Sydney. 1982. "The Inverted Spectrum." *Journal of Philosophy* 79, 7: 357–81.

Skorupski, John. 1989. *John Stuart Mill*. London: Routledge.

Soles, David E. 1998. "Locke on Ideas, Words, and Knowledge." *Revue International de Philosophie* 42: 150–72.

———. 1999. "*Is* Locke an Imagist?" *The Locke Newsletter* 30: 17–66.

Spencer, Thomas. 1628. *The Art of Logic*. London. Scolar Press facsimile.

Stillingfleet, Edward. 1697. *A Discourse in Vindication of the Doctrine of the Trinity: with an Answer to the Late Socinian Objections against it from Scripture, Antiquity and Reason*. London.

Swing, Thomas K. 1969. *Kant's Transcendental Logic*. New Haven: Yale University Press.

Taylor, C.C.W. 1978. "Berkeley's Theory of Abstract Ideas." *Philosophical Quarterly* 28, III: 1–19.

Thalberg, Irving. 1981. "The Discovery of Nonsense." In *Midwest Studies in Philosophy 6*, edited by Peter French, Theodore Uehling, and Howard Wettstein. Notre Dame, IN: University of Notre Dame Press.

Urmson, J.O. 1967. *Philosophical Analysis*. Oxford: Oxford University Press.

Walmsley, Jonathan. 1999. "Locke on Abstraction: A Response to M.R. Ayers." *British Journal for the History of Philosophy* 7: 123–34.

Weidemann, H. 1989. "Aristotle on Inferences from Signs." *Phronesis* 34: 343–51.

Winkler, Kenneth. 1989. *Berkeley: An Interpretation*. Oxford: Clarendon Press.

Wisdom, John. 1931–3. "Logical Constructions I–V." *Mind* 40–2.

Wittgenstein, Ludwig. 1953. *Philosophical Investigations*. Translated by G.E.M. Anscombe. New York: Macmillan.

———. 1958. *The Blue and Brown Books*. Translated by Rush Rhees. London: Blackwell.

———. 1974. *Tractatus Logico-Philosophicus*. Translated by D.F. Pears and Brian McGuinness. London: Routledge.

Woolhouse, Roger. 1972. *Locke's Philosophy of Science and Knowledge*. New York: Barnes and Noble.

Woozley, A.D. 1964. "Introduction." In *Locke's Essay Concerning Human Understanding*, edited by Woozley. New York: Meridian.

———. 1976. "Berkeley's Doctrine of Notions and Theory of Meaning." *Journal of the History of Philosophy* 14: 427–34.

Yolton, John. 1968. *John Locke and the Way of Ideas*. Cambridge: Cambridge University Press, 1968.

———. 1970. *Locke and the Compass of Human Understanding*. Cambridge: Cambridge University Press.

———. 1984. *Perceptual Acquaintance from Descartes to Reid*. Minneapolis: University of Minnesota Press.

———. 2000. "Response to My Fellow Symposiasts." In *Descartes' Natural Philosophy*, edited by Stephen Gaukroger, John Schuster, and John Sutton. London: Routledge.

Zemach, Eddy. 1976. "Putnam's Theory on the Reference of Substance Terms." *Journal of Philosophy* 73, 5: 116–27.

Index